BIBLICAL WOMEN
WHO CHANGED THE WORLD

Ancient Wisdom And Prophecy For Today

MELINDA RIBNER

BIBLICAL WOMEN
WHO CHANGED THE WORLD
Copyright © 2016 by Melinda Ribner

All rights reserved. No part of this book may be reproduced in any form or by any means—whether electronic, digital, mechanical, or otherwise—without permission in writing from the publisher, except by a reviewer, who may quote brief passages in a review.

World Ahead Press is a division of WND Books. The views and opinions expressed in this book are those of the author and do not necessarily reflect the official policy or position or WND Books.

Paperback ISBN: 978-1-944212-42-1
eBook ISBN: 978-1-944212-43-8

Printed in the United States of America
16 17 18 19 20 21 LSI 9 8 7 6 5 4 3 2 1

PRAISE FOR BIBLICAL WOMEN WHO CHANGED THE WORLD

"This beautiful and timely book restores the honor due to women with much deep spiritual wisdom for both women and men."
　　Rabbi Sholom Brodt, Director of Shlomo Yeshivah in Jerusalem.

"Melinda Ribner, one of the leading Torah teachers and spiritual guides of our time, has created a new genre in which, through her deep sensitivity to the subtle nuances of biblical texts and midrashim (oral tradition), we can take a fresh look at the great women of Israel not as statuesque figures from the past but as real people who responded heroically to actual life challenges . . . This work will empower women and enrich men with a wealth of insights that will help them to better understand the strength and greatness of their own mothers, wives, sisters, and daughters."
　　Rabbi Avraham Greenbaum, author of *On Wings of the Sun*.

"I was amazed how much knowledge Ribner as a Jewish woman shared about Biblical women in this book that I did not previously know. This book is beautifully written and is a wonderful teaching tool. It will inspire and empower Jewish and Christian women alike. It helped me better understand the person God created me to be."
　　Tammy Johnson, Divine Destiny Ministries in Geneva, NY.

"Ms. Ribner, in her book, Biblical Women Who Changed the World, seeks to introduce the reader to the notable women of Judaism by setting up a series of modern day interviews in order to plumb the depths of biblical wisdom in

a format to which post-modern reader can relate. Ribner weaves tradition, history and biblical texts into a tapestry that she uses to view issues of the day. From the role of women, to the unrest in the Middle East, she brings ancient wisdom to bear upon the anxieties of modern people.

After reading this book one will have a much stronger sense of the scope of Jewish tradition, the pivotal role played by the women of the Bible, and a renewed sense that that which was important in ancient times, remains important today. In a world that seems obsessed with making men and women alike, we read of the sacred feminine that defines the unique gifts women bring to the world, to their relationships and to their children. Ribner holds up the women of what was and, in some cases, still is, a highly patriarchal culture, reminding us of their pivotal role in the history of the Jews and, indeed, the world.

I would recommend this book to Christians who seek to better understand the traditions of ancient Judaism as expressed both in the Bible and other sources. In the midst of the interviews of Sarah, Ester and others, Ribner intersperses a wealth of information about the study of scripture, commentary, spirituality and the rich oral traditions of the Middle East and Egypt."

Deacon Dennis Lohouse serves the Rochester,
NY Catholic Diocese at St. Pius X Parish

"Melinda Ribner offers a fresh biblical perspective on women that Christians won't easily find elsewhere. To her credit, she seeks to "offer pathways of feminine empowerment different than that of feminism." Filled with nuggets of wisdom, women will be naturally attracted to this book to learn more about themselves. So, women, I urge you to read this book! But also, if you're a man who wants to understand the opposite sex better, you need to read this book too!"

Michael J. Klassen, Author, Pastor,
and World Ahead Press Acquisitions Director.

"I waited my whole life for a book that would elevate women like this holy book does. This is must reading for every girl and woman of all faiths, but it is equally important for men to read this book so as to increase their appreciation of the women in their lives."

Yitta Halberstam Mandelbaum, co-author of Small Miracles series.

PRAISE FOR BIBLICAL WOMEN WHO CHANGED THE WORLD

"Reb Mindy Ribner reads Scripture with profound knowledge, empathy, and intuition. She takes the reader into the imaginal world of the matriarchs and makes them love and speak to our time. It is a book of spiritual genius. "
   Rabbi Zalman Schacter-Shalomi of blessed memory.

"Melinda Ribner's book is a timely gift to a world that is re-examining the relationships between masculine and feminine forces that shape so much of our reality. Her writing is infused with vitality and passion and saturated with rich wisdom from the Jewish tradition, filtered through her own, most feminine being. Her words are urgently needed, not only by women, but by men who are striving to understand and honor the enduring interplay between the masculine and the feminine."
   Rabbi Daniel Raphael Silverstein, Hillel Rabbi, Stanford University.

DEDICATION

I dedicate this book to my sweet and beloved mother, Corinne Ribner of blessed memory, who left this world on July 30, 2009. That day happened to be Tisha B'Av, the Jewish holiday of mourning commemorating the destruction of the Holy Temples in Jerusalem. Just as the Holy Temple is the foundation of Jewish life, my mother was my foundation.

    I spoke to my mother almost every day. She would often end each telephone conversation with "I love you." When she would call me "my sweetheart," as she often did, and when she would smile toward me, I felt bathed in love. I thought I knew my mother. But it was only in her death and its aftermath that I glimpsed the real woman she was. Her courage, generosity of spirit, and the pure faith she displayed during her illness and dying was beyond anything I knew of her. Where did she have this strength? She always told me that she had a private relationship with God that sustained her since childhood.

My mother thought this book could be redemptive for all women, herself, and especially for me. She encouraged me to find my own voice as a woman. "Be courageous, brutally honest, and authentic. Do something important," she said to me. She admonished me when she thought I was too scholarly in the text, or sold out my voice as a woman in efforts to gain legitimacy in the male-dominated Torah world.

Like many women of my generation who embraced feminism, I had devalued the feminine and imitated men in an attempt to gain power and influence. I feared the economic dependence typical of women of my mother's generation. Admittedly, in my eventual pursuit of spiritual knowledge and growth, I ran to learn from one male rabbi to another, studied from books written by men, and did not value my mother's wisdom as much as I should have.

Only in the wake of her death did I realize that my mother was my greatest spiritual teacher—and my best friend, as she often reminded me. She transmitted to me a sublime "women's Torah" not found in books. All the while, she lovingly and patiently guided me to reclaim the feminine.

I wish I had acknowledged her more when she was alive. I pray for this book to be a testimony to my mother's strength and goodness. May the soul of my beloved mother smile from her heavenly station.

The biblical women in this book modeled for me how to stand courageous in this challenging world. I pray for this book to inspire others to share their appreciation and gratitude to their mothers, and to all women who gently embody the often-unappreciated love and depth that is unique to women.

* * *

This book is also dedicated to the other members of my family.

To my beloved, precious, and loving father Isaac Ribner of blessed memory; to my beloved awesome uncle Dr. Richard Ribner of blessed memory; to my beloved aunt, my father's oldest living sister, Bernice Rogow, an inspiring and living model of the feminine, 101 years old at the writing of this book; and to my dearest beloved brother Stephen Ribner, one of the most positive and loving men on the planet today.

CONTENTS

	Preface	10
	Introduction	14
1.	Eve's Gift of Love	17
2.	Sarah's Discernment	39
3.	Rebecca's Higher Truth	55
4.	Rachel, Leah, Bilha, and Zilpa	67
5.	Dina the Heroine	88
6.	Miriam's Vision	97
7.	Batya's Rebellion	117
8.	Chana's Prayer	127
9.	Queen Esther	139
10.	Meditations and Contemplations on the Divine Presence	157
11.	Biblical Prophecies and America's Fate	161
	Conclusion	176
	Postscript	180

PREFACE

There are precious moments in life when we receive guidance from deep within that alters our lives. These wake-up calls to our very souls can imprint upon us forever. We are different than we were before. This book evolved from such a personal holy moment.

I sat in a typical Saturday-afternoon Torah class when it happened. The rabbi shared a little known secret about the life and death of Sarah. Abraham and Isaac's faith to meet a great spiritual test is touted in the daily morning service in the Jewish prayer book, but little is told of Sarah's point of view as the wife, or as the mother of Isaac. I'd never before considered the impact of this story on Sarah, the mother.

When Sarah saw a vision of her husband planning to kill her precious son Isaac on Mount Moriah, she died of grief and anguish. This teaching from the Zohar (an ancient and the most prominent esoteric commentary on the Bible) postulates her last words to possibly have been, "Take me and not my son." As a prophetess, her words had the power to change reality. She died and her son lived.

The intensity of my emotional reaction to this untold story of the death of Sarah astonished me. Though I remained silent during the class, I screamed within. "How could Abraham be praised for meeting the greatest test of his life when it resulted in Sarah's death? Where was the sensitivity to a mother's heart? Weren't Sarah's feelings important?"

Her pain became my pain. What happened to her didn't feel as the distant past but more like the same lack of acknowledgement for the heart of the feminine still happening today. I identified with Sarah for this first time. Inspired by feminism in the 1970s and 1980s (in my twenties and thirties), I had tried hard to make it in a man's world. I wore pantsuits like Hillary Clinton and sported a leather briefcase just like my male colleagues. It was important to me that at least in work or in public I be taken seriously and not marginalized because I was a woman. I would even chide myself to think like a man rather than feel like a woman.

That afternoon, I was afraid to speak up to the rabbi and reveal my vulnerability. I had thought I might cry if I tried to speak. I feared being discounted or even ridiculed for my sensitive feminine heart. So much churned within me. I felt emotionally distressed, yet was inwardly exhilarated. I realized that women in the Bible like Sarah had something to teach me about being a woman, a Jew, a human being that I did not yet know and needed to know.

In that holy transformational moment, I received a new soul-mission to discover and share what I learned. I immediately envisioned a book revealing the deeper teachings not widely known about biblical women. This book would be a celebration of the heart and wisdom of the feminine, hidden in untold stories of biblical women, seen from a woman's perspective. I would claim my voice as a woman by writing this book. With tears in my eyes, I prayed to be worthy.

Before that day, I wasn't particularly interested in the stories of the Bible or in gender issues. Consequently, I hadn't investigated beyond the simple reading of the text. My primary focus was prayer, spiritual development, and healing. For more than twenty-five years, I taught Jewish meditation and wrote several books on the subject. My work focused on cultivating and sharing the direct experience of the holiness of God.

As I worked on this book, I came to understand my previous resistance towards the study of biblical women. I had accepted the standard interpretations of the Bible and had blamed biblical women for the chaos in the world. I accepted that the first woman, Eve, brought evil and death into the world for eating fruit from the Tree of Knowledge of Good and Evil and then sharing it with her husband. I blamed Sarah for causing the conflict in the Middle East between Arabs and Jews when she sent Ishmael, the spiritual head of the Muslims and his mother, Hagar away, an act against the will of her husband. There are too many biblical stories blaming women for me to recount them all here. I realized I didn't want to identify with these biblical women in the way they'd been presented to me.

After my Saturday Torah class, I returned home and pondered why Sarah's death made me so unbearably sad. I reflected why she had to die and what she might have experienced in the last moments of her life. I listened deep within for answers. Many times I meditated and contemplated on Sarah's life and death. I later repeated this process with the soul of other biblical women. I felt drawn to ask them questions and imagined them talking to me. I simply wrote down the guidance I received.

From deep reflection on the life of Sarah, I realized that she, the mother of the Jewish people, was not a victim who we should pity. Rather, it is incumbent upon us to honor Sarah as a brave heroine and our spiritual mother. She was not an elderly woman who simply died of a broken heart. History has not yet fully acknowledged the contribution Sarah made in safeguarding the life of her son and the vitality of the Jewish people. I made a pledge to Mother Sarah that I would be a mouthpiece, as best as I could be, for her and other biblical women whose stories are not fully heard.

I realized later that my tears and pain had arisen from a source deeper than Sarah's actual death. I came to understand that I cried for the *Shechinah*, the feminine face, the immanence of the Divine. Deeper study informed me that biblical women are considered embodiments of the Shechinah. I had cried for myself, for all women, and for the world.

My tears fell for the silenced feminine voice: for her unacknowledged wisdom, for her loving heart betrayed, and for her compromised freedom. Our world suffers from the diminishment of the feminine. Rather than feeling depleted after such a profound crying spell, I felt purified, invigorated, and blessed. These were holy tears, the kind that can awaken Divine blessing.

In this book, God is primarily called by two names. Even though the Jewish conception of the oneness of God is non-physical, neither male nor female, Judaism refers to God's two primary faces with these different names. The masculine face of God is referenced as "The Holy One Blessed be He," or *Ha Kodesh Boruch Hu*. The Hebrew word Kodesh means holy, referring to transcendent and separate from the world. The other name, Shechinah, the feminine face of the Divine, refers to the imminent and manifest Presence of God.

In most religions, God is commonly referred to in the masculine, such as 'Father who art in Heaven.' It made me wonder, if there is a father, is there not a mother? Where is She? Is God only in the sky? Is that why people are always looking upwards? Is God also not here on earth as well? This book aims to increase our awareness of the Shechinah, the immanence or Presence of God.

I had another holy moment, a "game-changer" that transformed and deepened my understanding of the feminine. I had a profound revelation of the Shechinah while praying near the Wailing Western Wall in Israel. After I began writing this book, I spent several months praying before each sunrise near the *Kodesh Kodeshim* in the tunnels excavated by the Wailing Western Wall in the Old City of Jerusalem. Considered the Holy of Holies, it is closest to the holiest place of the ancient Holy Temple in Jerusalem. I was privileged to pray there, surrounded by the holy men and women of Jerusalem daily.

It may sound crazy, but I felt as though She, the Shechinah, spoke to me. I was informed of the following: God's covenant with the Jewish people is real. In the right time, all the prophecies will be revealed. I intuitively understood that the Shechinah is eternally united with Hakodesh Borechu. But when our hearts are open, it is She who gives us a glimpse of God's profound beauty and faithful love. This revelation of the Shechinah strengthens and sustains us until the great messianic day when God will be fully revealed throughout the world. In those future glorious times, our hearts, minds and souls will then know God and our unity with each other. There will then be true peace and everlasting joy. Evil will have no jurisdiction. This book is dedicated to that revelation of God.

I conclude with this blessing:

May all who seek to know God be blessed with many holy moments when it is clear that there is a God who loves them unconditionally. Just as I received a wake-up call to write this book, may everyone receive guidance and gentle wake-up calls to fulfill their unique life purpose. May the light of our awakened God-consciousness illuminate the darkness in the world.

INTRODUCTION

Biblical women were allotted very few words in the Bible, yet they changed the world forever. Often in opposition to the will and desire of their husbands, they made choices that embodied the heart and wisdom of the feminine. These choices altered the future history of their progeny, with an indelible impact on the world at large as well. This book celebrates the important contributions made by biblical women to safeguard and strengthen all that is precious in our world.

Biblical women are important for more than what they did to change the world in ancient times. Their stories are important for what they offer us today. Their prophecies help us understand and respond to current world events. The Bible is still relevant because people face challenges similar to that of our ancestors.

The life stories of biblical women represent soul-archetypes of courageous and transformational forces. By making choices today in spiritual alignment with them, we continue their holy redemptive work. As prophetesses, biblical women model how we can transform ourselves and make our homes and our communities dwelling places for God. This is the most important work we must do today.

* * *

This book was previously published under the title *The Secret Legacy of Biblical Women*, with a different emphasis and goal. I chose to publish this special edition of the book in order to reach Christian communities. Jews and Christians today face common enemies sworn to our persecution. Through Divine providence, we are brought together in a way like never before.

This edition contains a new chapter focusing on the connection between current world events and biblical prophecies. I expand upon the prophecies of biblical women previously revealed in the interviews to make a case for change in America's direction—for its own sake.

The heart of this book remains the imaginary interview format with biblical women. Each biblical woman tells her story and speaks to the needs of people today. While these interviews are an outpouring of my soul and heart, my intention is to communicate little-known teachings from the Zohar and other esteemed rabbinic commentaries. Please know that I do not profess to be a channel or an intermediary of any sort. These interviews are intended to serve as a springboard for thinking and discussion. This text may be seen by many as having a radical construct because biblical women were not "politically correct."

This book aims to highlight the innate gifts bestowed upon women and offer pathways for feminine empowerment different than that of feminism. While feminism emphasizes egalitarianism as a way to assure fairness between the sexes, this book celebrates the differences between men and women.

Biblical women served in leadership positions not by imitating men, but by embodying the unique qualities of the feminine. The world today is in dire need of such women. The Talmud, the rabbinical commentary of the Bible, teaches that it was only due to the merit of women that the Jewish people were able to leave Egypt in ancient times. It is also taught by many rabbis that women will lead the world forward to the messianic age. "The final redemption will be due to the merit of the righteous women of that generation" (Yalkut Shimoni Ruth)

Where will this essential female leadership come from if women do not claim their unique voice and power as women? This book offers individual and group practices for women to heighten their innate spiritual power to expand their healing, loving influence in the world today.

Feminism may have opened the gates to the workplace for women, but it cannot galvanize or empower women spiritually. Feminism arose out of communist theology and secular humanism and is non-theistic and anti-theistic rather than God-centered. For those of us who recognize God as the source and center of our life, it is preferable to reclaim our innate spiritual gifts and empowerment as women, much like our biblical mothers before us.

I am writing this book because of my deep appreciation of the love and support given to the Jewish State of Israel by the global Christian community. I understand that this support is a pure expression of Christian faith and a love of the Bible. That is fine with me. I pray that our difficult past does not stand in the way of uniting us today. We need each other like never before. We face common enemies sworn to our mutual annihilation. I am happy that we are being brought together today.

Jews and Christians alike wait for the Messiah. Our faiths recognize that world problems are too large for human beings to solve on our own. As my rabbi friend remarked before an audience of Christian clergy when sharing Jewish teachings about the Messiah, "Let us not argue about the identity of the Messiah now. In the future it will be clear. From my part, it will be one Jew or another."

A little humor is always helpful.

CHAPTER ONE

EVE'S GIFT OF LOVE
SECRETS OF HOLY INTIMACY

A woman lives for love. This is good, and a sign of her strength and not a weakness. In her heart of hearts, a woman cannot tolerate superficiality. So honor your depths. Yearn to surrender and be penetrated with Godliness. This is a greatest joy.

—*Eve, The Mother of all Life*

EVE (CHAVA)
THE FIRST WOMAN, MOTHER OF ALL LIVING

Upon a simple reading of the Bible, many blame Eve (woman) for bringing evil and death into the world. As the story goes, Eve ate the forbidden fruit then gave it to Adam to eat. The punishments for this "sin" were metered out to all accordingly. Adam and Eve were cast out of the Garden of Eden. The serpent that tempted the woman was cursed to crawl on its belly, eat dust, and have enmity between itself and womankind for all time. Because of Eve's action, a woman would now experience pain in childbirth, she will need her husband more than her husband will need her, and her husband would rule over her. And in recourse of man listening to the voice of his wife, he now has to work by the "sweat of his brow" to survive.

Others reject this biblical story as misogynistic—a story written by men to justify the oppression of women. Yes, it is true that women have been oppressed and man has had to work for his "bread," and the serpent crawls on the ground. But is there a deeper reading of this story?

According to Jewish esoteric wisdom, the secrets of creation and all future events are encoded in this story of Adam and Eve. Whether we take the story literally or metaphorically is not so important. It is important to understand the wisdom contained within this story. First, we need to know this story and all the commentaries about it, so as to enter into it and allow it to become our story as well.

The story of Eve, the first woman, is known in Hebrew as Chava, the "Mother of All Living," and is the archetype for women of all times.

ADAM AND EVE WERE INITIALLY A SINGLE NONPHYSICAL BEING!
The Bible tells us that Eve and Adam were originally one being, called "Adam."

"Let us make man in our image, after our likeness . . . So God created man in his image, in the image of God He created him, male and female He created them" (Gen. 1:27).

Creation began with one being, Adam, so all people would know that they have the same creator. Adam, the original being, contained the souls of all people, men and women of all nations, for all generations to come. Today, you too are a part of this original being known as Adam.

The first instructions to this bi-gendered being were to be fruitful, multiply, and rule over the fish, the birds, and every living thing (Gen. 1:28). Since Adam was both male and female when receiving these instructions, it would appear that Adam could reproduce asexually. Adam was originally placed outside of the Garden of Eden and then taken within the Garden to work and guard it (Gen. 2:15). Adam was then instructed to freely eat of all the trees except the fruit of the Tree of Knowledge of Good and Evil, for if he were to eat of this fruit, he would die (Gen. 2:17).

"It is not good to be alone," God says. "I will make him a helper (*ezrah genedo*), opposite him" (Gen. 2:18).

According to Jewish legends, Adam was given Lilith to help Adam overcome his feelings of isolation. This occurred prior to the creation of Eve. Lilith is not mentioned in the Bible, but is prominent in the Zohar and in the Talmud. Lilith also appears in ancient Sumerian mythology as well as in other surrounding ancient cultures.

Lilith was created separately from Adam and never assumed bodily form like Adam did after "the fall." The legend is that Lilith insisted on full equality and consequently abandoned Adam because Adam was unwilling to yield to her demands. With the use of the ineffable name, Lilith flew to the Red Sea, away from Adam. Lilith, said to be spurned by Adam, is still overcome with jealousy of humankind, and capable of injuring babies. Even to this day, people secure amulets to protect infants from her.

According to the Bible, the best helpmate that Adam needed would not be separate from Adam, but would come directly from him. This woman was always there, they were one being; they were adjoined back to back, and she was never noticed. She was to be separated from the body of Adam. It was part of the Divine plan from the beginning that they would be separated, but it was important that they first share the memory of being part of one being. Such a deep connection did not develop between Lilith and Adam because they did not share a common root.

God cast a deep sleep upon Adam and took one of his sides (Gen. 2:21). And man said, "*This time* it is bone of my bones and flesh of my flesh. This shall be called woman, for from man was she taken" (Gen. 2:24). Now man and woman stood separate from each other, face to face, so as to now be able to help and challenge each other to grow. Adam expresses his approval. Eve is silent.

The main act attributed to Eve was that she ate from the Tree of Knowledge of Good and Evil. God had commanded Adam to not eat of this Tree. Adam told Eve to not eat or even touch the Tree, but Eve ate and then gave the fruit to Adam to eat. When Adam and Eve did eat of the Tree of Knowledge of Good and Evil, the evil that was formerly outside of them was now incorporated into their very being. Everything now in the world, as within every man and woman, would contain a mixture of good and evil. And, there may be times when it is no longer easy to distinguish between the two. As a result of eating of the Tree of Knowledge of Good and Evil, Adam and Eve, and all of humanity henceforth are endowed the responsibility to make choices between good and evil. When God questions both of them after eating, each one fails to take responsibility for what they had done.

In my interview with Eve, she will explain many of her motivations for eating of the Tree. Consider how her arguments resonate with you. Some of the deepest esoteric wisdom is incorporated into this interview.

For information about Eve, read excerpts in Genesis 2:22–23, 3:2–3, 3:7, 3:20, 3:22, and 4:1.

INTERVIEW WITH EVE

It is awesome to be in your presence. What is your message for the women of today?
Eve: I love you and I bless you. You are a part of me as I am within you. You may feel that you have your own personal identity but you are much more than you know yourself to be. You may also feel that you are no different than a man, because in your present world you can do everything that a man can do and more. Know firsthand, always remember, and be mindful that you are a woman. As a woman, you have a special and unique mission in the world. You are beautiful. You are powerful. There is much that you as a woman must do to bring this world into the proper balance and harmony. Please know that women share a bond that cannot yet be totally revealed. My heart is full of blessing for everyone. May this revelation of the feminine occur as soon as possible.

Thank you for that wonderful introduction and blessing. Would you please begin by telling us about yourself?
Eve: In the first story of creation recorded in the Bible, Adam and I were created as one being. We were joined together, yet we did not face each other, we were back to back in a state of unconsciousness. We were not really connected, or close to each other. A slumber fell upon Adam and I was then created as a separate conscious entity.

After I was separated from Adam, my size was reduced. I was smaller, and was conscious of life in a different way than he was. I needed him and he needed me. I stood opposite him, so as to stimulate and challenge him. I knew that if I did my job well, I would be restored to my full stature. I could then face Adam in a loving relationship of mutuality and respect. This is what I wanted the most. It has been my hope and prayer from the beginning of time that my original size will be restored and I would stand face to face in a full loving relationship with my husband.

But why did you do it, Eve? Why did you eat from the Tree of the Knowledge of Good and Evil?
Eve: Like women throughout the ages, I have always been guided throughout my life by the desire for love and relationship. Men like to love, but love is life to a woman. There is a deep yearning in the heart of the feminine for love. Please know this about me when you seek to understand why I did what I did.

I know that I have been blamed for bringing sin into the world. I have been blamed for bringing chaos and death into the world. My action has regrettably been used to oppress women. The suffering endured by women of all cultures throughout time is an unfortunate legacy, a profound burden, and even a sacrifice, that women, including myself, have borne since the beginning of time.

My legacy will be redeemed in the future. What I did and what women have done for all of humanity has not yet been understood nor fully appreciated. I know the truth will become clear in the right time. When it is understood, all of humanity will have profound appreciation and respect for me and for all women. All will know that what I did was necessary to move life forward. May my legacy be redeemed in your time.

Does not the Bible say, "Of every tree of the garden you may eat, but of the Tree of the Knowledge of Good and Evil, you must not eat, for if you eat of it, you will die" (Gen. 2: 16–17)? Adam even told you to not eat of the Tree or even touch it.
Eve: Firstly, Adam had been given the prohibition against eating of the Tree when he was alone, before I was created. Because we were back to back at that time, I did not hear this command directly. After I came on to the scene as a separate entity, life had radically changed for us, offering us new possibilities. It was now a new order and together we could do more than before. When I touched the Tree inadvertently because the serpent pushed me against it, and nothing happened, I

did not know whether I could believe Adam. When I ate the outside of the fruit and also nothing happened, I then ate the whole fruit. My consciousness was radically altered. There was a painful separation between me and Adam then, so I gave him the fruit and we were united again.

You did not yet answer the question, Eve. Why did you do it? Why did you eat from the Tree of the Knowledge of Good and Evil? I want to understand your motivation.

Eve: My goal was for knowledge of God, for union with the Divine. Without this God knowledge, my life was empty and meaningless. The fruit looked good and I knew it would make one wise. The serpent told me that my eyes would be open and I would be like God knowing good and evil. As the helpmate to Adam, it was clear to me that my job was to stimulate Adam to grow in his knowledge and service of God. I wanted him to more fully realize his awesome potential and do what he was created to do. It is the nature of woman to stimulate man to grow. Without this stimulation from the woman, man would not develop.

Adam was a great, even a magnificent being of light, but I knew that was only because he was created that way. He didn't do anything to earn or deserve what he had. He simply received all the wondrous light that was so generously bestowed upon him. More importantly, while he was joyfully basking in the light, there were sparks of Divine light trapped in darkness. It was his job to restore these sparks to their source, but he was blinded by his own light and could not perceive darkness. Because I was diminished myself, I felt the pain acutely of not being unified with the Holy One. It was my job to inspire Adam to do what he was supposed to do and to be all that he could be.

Please explain.

Eve: Adam had been given the responsibility of tending all that was in the Garden. By doing this holy work, Adam and I would merit the light that was so lovingly and completely shining upon us. As a woman, I knew more than Adam how important it was that we participate and earn what is given to us. To just receive is shameful. We can't just take and take and not give back. I understood that by eating of the Tree, our consciousness would change, but we would be able to give and to love in a deeper way. Life would not be easy, I knew that, but life without change, life without love is not meaningful to me. In my heart I believed that what I did was what God originally wanted. God did not want

Adam and me to be simply puppets with no free will. That is why God placed the Tree in our midst.

Eve, you make it sound like the eating was a good thing. How can that be? You brought sin into the world and with it suffering and death. It was a sin, wasn't it?

Eve: I understand that this act has been considered a sin by most people. Some people even call it the original sin and believe that all evil in the world is derived from this one act. Perhaps we should have waited until *Shabbat,* but my love for all of creation was too large. The cosmic residue of light, the fallen sparks that were left out of the garden, were calling out for love and healing. They experienced a profound immeasurable pain from their disconnection from God. There is no greater pain than this. I was willing to personally enter into the darkness, into what you call evil, for the sake of love. Such is the nature of a woman who loves. Women do this all the time.

You make it sound like this act was completely altruistic. Was there another motivation underlying your decision to eat of the forbidden tree?

Eve: Ultimately, quite honestly, I wanted to bring Adam closer to me. I knew that as Adam developed, we would be better able to be together in a more direct and complete way. The kind of relationship that he could have with me would be much different and better than he could have with Lilith. His desire for Lilith was based entirely on the desire for physical pleasure and nothing else. Yet Adam was still, however, spending time with Lilith, playing with her and wasting his seed with her. I was alone too much of the time. This is why the serpent could approach me and try to seduce me.

What was your relationship with the serpent?

Eve: Adam had befriended the serpent and let him spend a lot of time with me. The serpent awakened lust within me. He injected his impurity into me. At the time, I did not know nor understand what was happening to me when I was with him. The serpent was the male version of Lilith. Since Adam desired Lilith so much, I hoped that my contact with the dark energy of the serpent would make me more attractive to Adam. More than anything, I wanted to attract Adam to me, so we could do what the Holy One wanted us to do, to procreate and fill the world with light and children. Regrettably I absorbed some of the filth of the serpent and then transferred it to my children, especially to Cain. I never loved the serpent. I only loved Adam. Adam is my eternal soul mate. My relationship with the serpent was only a means to fulfill a holy purpose.

Eve, was it not a sin? Did you not do something wrong? Were not you, Adam, and even the serpent punished?
Eve: On the surface reading of the Bible, it looks like we were each punished in very specific ways. In actuality the punishments ascribed to us were exactly what we needed to heal and fulfill us on the deepest level. The Holy One never punishes, but rather the Holy One fulfills the desires of all. Everything that the Holy One does is for good. What happens to a person is always what is needed for growth. I accept and rejoice in that truth, and so should you.

Let's look at the punishments: that man should suffer through his labor and that woman should suffer during her labor. What is labor but manifestation of co-creativity? Please know that what God ordained was good for us. It was what we really needed. It was not only good for Adam to work, it was essential for him to work in order to earn life in this world and "The World to Come." Adam needed to work rather than spend his time chasing Lilith. There is no merit without toil. As it is said in the holy writings, "In proportion to the toil is the reward." After the "sin" he now was finally clear about the importance of his mission to make this world a dwelling place for the Divine.

What about the curse of pain in childbirth? Women still suffer from the pain of childbirth.
Eve: After the eating of the Tree of the Knowledge of Good and Evil, I was given the name Chava, which means "Mother of All Living." What an honor and privilege! Previously I was simply called woman. I did not have a real name. Now I was elevated to the holy status of mother. If it was really such a sin, why would I be rewarded with this glorious name?

Regarding the punishment of pain in childbirth, people assume that pain is bad, but pain is not bad if it is serving a positive and holy purpose. Life is all good. The pain of childbirth is particularly exquisite for it cracks open the heart, soul, and body of a woman so she receives a higher and more profound revelation of God. Through giving birth, a woman becomes like God. She is the creator of life. After the pain of childbirth, she is better able to mother her child as this child has come through her.

Birthing, like much of life, is not something a woman can control, but something she must allow to take place within her and through her. When a woman learns to relax, trust, and ride the wave of bodily sensations during birthing, she is filled with awe. She bears witness directly to the Divine Mother's holy work taking place within her. If a woman becomes very frightened when giving birth, there will be more pain than necessary. A woman's pain in childbirth and life in general diminishes when she learns to surrender to that which is greater than herself.

Always remember, dear women, to relax, let go, and be open to the love that flows through you simply by virtue of being a woman. Please keep your beautiful heart open, even when you are sad and frightened. It is much better to feel the depth of your feelings, breathe through them and release them rather than build a hard shell around your sensitive and beautiful heart that will only block off the flow of love to you. Your safety paradoxically lies in your openness, your vulnerability and willingness to surrender to the depths of who you are.

At her very core, every woman must learn not to resist life but rather to courageously and open-heartedly embody the beauty of life and the awesomeness of God for all to see. The Divine Mother is revealed through every woman, whether she is birthing a child, nurturing relationships, or involved in creative projects that foster greater connectivity and love in her world. When a woman opens herself to embody Her, she will feel ecstatically joyful and grateful for the awesome gifts and even the challenges that have been given to her as a woman.

What about your husband "ruling" over you? That doesn't sound good to me.

Eve: This was also not a punishment. I actually wanted Adam to "rule" over me. What need does a woman have of a man if she does not allow him to offer her direction? When a woman allows a man to demonstrate leadership, they are both uplifted. When a woman is honoring of her man, he actually becomes more honorable. I know that may not sound politically correct to many women and men in your modern time. Please understand that I did not want to be independent like Lilith. Neither do most women in their heart of hearts. It is quite simple. A woman was created to receive from a man. She has been blessed with a womb that is a portal to the Divine. Her very womb is an internal compass to guide her forward as a woman. She will draw the right man toward her if she only listens and allows the arousal to occur within her.

Within the womb of most women is a deep hunger for a man, a soul mate, and ultimately a husband. To this man a woman will joyfully open, surrender, and allow him to enter her, penetrate, and permeate her with light and love. The feminine heart yearns for this depth of love. That is the main reason why I ate of the Tree. Adam was a great light. Even angels worshipped him. Adam was my husband and soul mate, so naturally I yearned to open myself to him. When my husband was giving to me, it was good for both of us, and we were both happy and joyful.

How is your story relevant to people today?
Eve: Because each man has a bit of Adam's light and each woman has a bit of my love, when they come together, they can experience the same joy that we did. Marital relations are a kind of re-union, through which men and women not only remember, they return and reclaim the original state of oneness that Adam and I had. The experience of oneness makes men and women very happy and the world is uplifted as well. Remember, the key to joy and fulfillment for a woman lies in her surrender, in her openness, her willingness to be vulnerable, to receive, and share.

It sounds like you are recommending that women be subordinate to men.
Eve: Oh, you clearly do not understand what I am saying at all! Ruling does not mean dominating or controlling. A man who is connected to the Divine and living to his potential is a true giver. It is his joy and it is his nature to provide direction for the woman and to give or, so to speak, rule with generosity. As I said earlier, within the heart and body of most women is the desire to receive from a man she can trust to give to her the highest light of God. Such a woman yearns to become impregnated with light and love, to nurture and grow it within her, so as to give the world something infinitely greater than what she had received. Our very anatomy reveals these deeper secrets. For example, a man gives a drop of semen, and a woman receives it, transforms it, and then gives the world an infant human being, created in the image and likeness of the Divine. Need I say more?

When a woman opens and truly allows herself to surrender and receive the Divine light her husband gives her by his very being and all that he does, she is then also better able to nurture herself and others. Everything around her comes alive and blossoms through her nurturing. Such a woman has a special radiance. When a woman is happy, her husband is happy, her children are happy.

What about men who are not so generous? There are men who are cruel to women. Should women allow themselves to be subordinate to them?
Eve: If a man does not demonstrate the capacity to be a bestower of light and love, there is no reason for a woman to remain with him. Of course, she must never allow herself to remain in a relationship where she is abused or even feels less than her husband. There is no holy purpose in that.

A man who seeks to dominate and control a woman, rather than give the light of his God consciousness to her, is disconnected from the Holy One. He pretends to be strong, but he is actually insecure and weak. He secretly fears and may be even jealous of the inherent spiritual beauty, awesome power, and Godliness of a woman. This kind of a man is actually more concerned with receiving than giving. No matter how masculine he may externally appear to be, he is more like a female than a man. But unlike a beautiful woman, his receiving is not for the sake of giving, so he is further weakened by his own selfishness, rather than strengthened. Only when a man becomes a giver is he strengthened.

What about religions that are oppressive to women? Should women simply accept their second-class status?
Eve: Unfortunately, it is true that there are manmade religions or aspects of true religions that are oppressive to women. Rather than honoring and elevating women, they treat them as second-class citizens. These religions even blame me for their evil actions. This is their projection and I am not responsible for that. They must know that when they do not honor, love and cherish women, they do not act in ways that are pleasing to the Holy One and the Shechinah, the Divine Feminine/Presence. The Holy One loves women and chose the woman to be the channel to bring life into the world. Is this not an honor and privilege?

Is there additional advice on this topic that you would like to give to women at this time? Many women are angry and suffer from low self-esteem because of mistreatment.
Eve: As a general rule, a woman must never allow herself to be defined by those who negate her intrinsic beauty and seek to subjugate her. Look at me; people throughout time have said such evil things about me. Follow in my footsteps and be unafraid. Please do not allow yourself to be affected by those who seek to denigrate you simply because you are a woman. It is a big mistake for a woman to judge herself by the criteria of a predominantly masculine culture that honors the qualities of the masculine and the diminishment of the feminine. In societies that value power over love, a woman might easily feel embarrassed, even ashamed, because she feels more deeply than a man. This is wrong. The beautiful loving heart of a woman is a Divine gift, a blessing to all and must be cherished rather than ridiculed.

Women, please remember your true beauty and your power lies in your willingness to embody the light and the loving heart of the Shechinah. No one can take that away from you, though they may try. Delight in being a loving, beautiful woman. If you suffer from low self-esteem, it is only because you have not internalized this truth sufficiently. Being a woman must be celebrated continually. Being a woman is a privilege.

How did you feel when Adam blamed you for eating of the Tree? Did you not feel betrayed?

Eve: I was so happy when Adam ate of the fruit I gave him to eat. He expressed his love for me by eating of the fruit so we would once again be united with each other. But when the Holy One questioned him, he blamed me for the change in his consciousness. I was very disappointed in Adam. I could no longer trust him. Yes, I did feel betrayed. He showed himself to be weak by blaming me, his wife, even if what he said was true.

Does what happened between you and Adam affect men and women today?

Eve: Yes, it does, unfortunately. It is important for both men and women to understand the effect. Because Adam blamed me as he did, there is still a residue of concern within all women throughout time—whether they can trust men. Will a man be strong enough to stand up for love, for truth? All women ponder this question and even at times test their men.

Similarly, because I gave to Adam to eat from the forbidden tree, I have come to understand that many men are still afraid of a woman's depths. And they have difficulty loving them because of it. Due to their own feelings of inadequacy and insecurity, men may even be jealous of and threatened by women's innate spiritual power.

So much healing needs to happen between men and women. When the healing between men and women is complete, there will be peace in the world.

You had three children with Adam. One of them, Cain, slew his twin brother Abel.

Eve: Regrettably, Cain was jealous and angry when his offerings were rejected and his brother's were accepted. He did not and could not appreciate the difference between the two offerings. Whereas Cain offered a small amount of the inferior portions of his crop—actually the leftovers after he had eaten—Abel had offered the finest of his flock before enjoying any personal benefit. Is there not a difference? Cain was arrogant and selfish and Abel was humble and generous. As a result, Abel's flock prospered and Cain's produce dwindled, which only added to Cain's feelings of jealousy.

Because he was the firstborn, Cain felt a sense of entitlement that he would rule over Abel. The Holy One warned Cain directly about the power of jealousy leading to sin and gave him the opportunity to change and do better. But Cain was so consumed with anger he could not hear this Divine call for repentance.

As his mother, I want you to know that Cain did not mean to kill Abel. It was not his fault. If it was anyone's fault, it was mine. Cain did not know that there would be death as a result of his actions. We had never witnessed death before. My son Cain unfortunately contained within him much of the serpent's sperm remaining in my body from my encounter with the serpent. He was not really the son of Adam. He didn't resemble him at all. Abel was also not entirely Adam's son either, though he contained less of the serpent's sperm.

Abel's death was a great loss to me. Adam deserted me rather than comforting me during this time of tragedy. He left me for one-hundred-thirty years. During this time period, he consorted with Lilith, creating demons and the souls of people who would incarnate later but would not be blessed with pure living Divine soul. These souls have incarnated into human bodies throughout time and cause great evil in the world. These people may look human, but they are not fully human. These evil souls continue to live and cause chaos even in your time. These souls, whether they inhabit Jewish bodies or not, can be known by their antipathy to the Jewish people.

Adam left you for one-hundred-thirty years!

Eve: Yes. Even though Adam deserted me for one-hundred-thirty years, I waited patiently for him to return to me. I did not return to the serpent. I knew that Adam would eventually come back to me because it was Divine Will that we would be together. We are soul mates. Adam did eventually return to me and I birthed Seth, who was the perfect expression of our union. Seth was born with the likeness of Adam, not like my other previous children. The children of Seth would carry on our mission of perfecting the world. Adam and I gave everything we knew to Seth.

Many women today are still waiting to be united with their soul mate. Do you have some words for them?

Eve: My heart is with women who are not married or in a bad marriage in which they are not loved. I know this pain intimately. It is truly heartbreaking that so many women and men are not wedded to their true soul mate. When a man and woman are married to their proper soul mate and engage in marital relations, they bring oneness into the world and reveal the Shechinah, the Divine Presence, in their midst. Because each woman contains a part of me and each man contains a part of Adam, every marriage restores the union between Adam and me. Every marriage has the possibility of bringing good and healing to the world.

When there is a breakdown in marriages, improper sexual relationships, or there are many lonely single people, disharmony is brought to the world. It is not good. Men are given the commandment to marry. They need it. It is more within the nature of a woman to marry. They do not need the commandment to marry.

Do you have any guidance for a woman?
Eve: Generally speaking, a woman is naturally more evolved and sensitive than a man. She loves more deeply and knows how integral love and relationship are in life. Women must be patient and do whatever they can to help men evolve. That is what I did and continue to do through women today.

The heart of a woman, whether single or married, is still patiently waiting and even yearning for the time when she can gracefully receive the light of the highest consciousness. A woman finds her fulfillment in the act of surrender to life, to the beloved one, found in her soul mate, human and Divine. An open loving heart is the most joyful way to live.

Not all women are so spiritual or patient nor do they want to surrender and be submissive as you recommend.
Eve: Yes, that is true. For some women, Lilith is more of their ideal than I am. They admire the rebelliousness of Lilith and her ability to challenge Adam. Many of these women who embody the Lilith energy in your day celebrate their independence and pride themselves on all their accomplishments. This, however, is not the truth of a woman's heart. A woman's independence will ultimately not fulfill her. Rather than live openly and gracefully as I advocate, Lilith-identified women try to control reality. Their own needs and desires are too often foremost in their minds. They simply do not know how to receive from the universe. Consequently, they feel inwardly angry, bitter, critical and resentful.

Truth be told, they are more about taking and manipulating others for their own selfish purposes than sharing the beauty and goodness of life with others. Is there not a difference between receiving in order to share and simply taking solely for one's own benefit?

Women who embody Lilith qualities may be beautiful and know how to use their sexuality in order to successfully seduce men, like Lilith, but they cannot love them nor do they want to love them or even receive love from them. Love requires vulnerability and surrender and that is too frightening to these women. There is a protective shell around their hearts that does not allow them to experience the surrender and joy of love. There is an unfortunate legacy of the wounded and defensive feminine that has been transmitted from mother to daughter throughout the generations.

What can women do to heal their defensiveness?

Eve: All women need to be sweetened by love, both human and Divine. A woman must know this about herself. Without this sweetening, she will be embroiled in negativity and be unable to free herself. By strengthening her connection to the Divine through prayer, meditation, and doing good deeds, she will be opened to receive the love of the Shechinah. A woman must learn to surrender to love and not to her fears. Love has the power to shatter the invisible energetic walls around her heart. Fear will only imprison her even more. By opening her heart and allowing herself to be vulnerable, a woman learns to trust and love herself, life itself, and God. The beauty of a woman lies in her receptivity, openness, and vulnerability, and not in her neediness or fearfulness.

When she is sufficiently healed, her open loving heart and light will draw to her a trustworthy man who can give her the love and pleasure she was created to receive. Until she has been sweetened by Divine love, she must, however, be discriminating in her relationships with men. Not all men are worthy of her trust.

A man may be equally self-serving and disconnected from the Divine as she is. Yet, when she discovers the power of love within her, she can be vulnerable because she knows that her safety truly comes from God. Her vulnerability becomes a gift she can offer to others. She no longer fears love, but knows, deep in her heart, that she has been bestowed with a beautiful loving heart to heal a particular man, those around her, as well as herself.

What should we learn from your story?

Eve: Do not lose faith. Remember deep within that life is intrinsically good. Beyond the labels of good and evil, beyond pain and betrayal, there is only good. Everything is good. Before we ate from the Tree of the Knowledge of Good and Evil, there was only good. The way to return to the consciousness of the Garden of Eden is to see all of life as good and make choices that reflect the goodness of life.

Do not take life for granted. Life in the physical world is precious because it does not last forever. You can recreate life in the Garden of Eden in the special moments of love you share with others. I know that life in the physical world is not easy, but it is nevertheless a great gift and privilege. Always remember that.

Do you have a particular closing message for women today?

Eve: Keep your heart open. As a woman, you have much to teach man about love and surrender, and how to truly serve God. Most men do not live and feel as deeply as you do. They are often not even aware of the lack of depth in their lives. A man is more governed by his routines, his habits, and his thoughts rather than his heart. A woman lives for love. This is good and a sign of her strength and not a weakness. In her heart of hearts, a woman cannot tolerate superficiality, so honor your depths. Yearn to surrender and be penetrated with Godliness. This is the greatest joy.

You are innately beautiful. Honor the Divine gifts that you have been given as a woman. When you open to the Shechinah, the Divine Feminine Presence, you may embody Her and radiate Her love to all you meet. Know that when you are with your man in holiness in sexual intimacy, you bring peace and harmony to the world. Keep yourself beautiful and attract a man to you. Without the arousal of the feminine, man would do very little in this world. You cannot overestimate the influence you have upon your man, your children, friends, and the world at large.

What about a closing message for men today?

Eve: A man is like the sun brilliantly shining light upon all—that is, when he is plugged into the Divine. Such a man is focused, assertive, disciplined, and heroic if need be. Like a decisive and fearless warrior, he can stand up courageously to all kinds of challenges and obstacles. His word is his pledge. He can be counted on to carry through with what he has committed to do. He walks his talk. He takes responsibility for his life and never blames anyone for his weaknesses and seeming failures, particularly his wife. Such a man is a wondrous being, worthy of a woman's love and adoration. If you inhabit a male body, strive to be this kind of man.

As a man, know that you will be tested in life, even by your own wife. As you pass these tests, you earn respect for yourself and from others. Let your word really mean something. Do not be hesitant to work hard. You came into this world to overcome evil, to do good, and to transform this world into a dwelling place for God. You will do this best when you are married.

If you are married, honor, cherish, appreciate, and love your wife. Like a beautiful flower, your wife needs your love to blossom. Little gestures mean so much to her. If you do actions that reflect these intentions, you will be worshipped by her. If you are not yet married, pray that you be guided to find your true soul mate, the one who will help you to be all that you can be, and then go out to find her in any way you must.

Also, give yourself time to be alone each day, to strengthen your inherent love connection with The Holy One Blessed be He. God is ready to give you all the strength you need to live your life powerfully. Meditate, pray, and learn each day. Do a physical spiritual practice as well.

My final blessing and prayer is that women and men come together to rejoice in love and transform this world into the paradise it was intended to be.

CONCLUDING RESPONSE TO MOTHER EVE

(It is suggested that this be read out loud by the reader or group.)

Mother Eve, thank you for your wisdom and your love. We have learned so much about the beauty and heart of the feminine from you. Most importantly, we have learned how to honor and cherish the feminine within ourselves and the world. We now identify more with the moon than the sun. Like the ever-changing moon, we as women demonstrate to all the art of openness and receiving, and a willingness to change and grow.

It is our nature and joy to be beautiful holy vessels that draw to us the love and light we need to be creative in this world. We are no longer ashamed of our vulnerability and longing for love and God. We were created for love. We create through love. We are not afraid of the power of our love. We do not fear love. Our hearts are so full of love. We are dedicated to increasing this love by sharing with others. We will safeguard our homes, our relationships and our mother earth.

Like you, Mother Eve, we are not afraid to enter into places of darkness within ourselves and others for the sake of love. May we each do our part in redeeming the Shechinah from Her hiddenness and exile, so the world will be a better place because of our love.

PRAYER TO THE GOD OF MOTHER EVE (CHAVA)

May the God of Mother Eve grant me the vision, the courage, and the strength to enter into places of darkness so as to heal and redeem what is wounded, and what is hidden, within me, others, and the world. May I be blessed to help restore all I encounter to a greater light, openness, and love.

What Quality of the Feminine Does Eve Demonstrate?

Eve stated succinctly, "Love is life to a woman," in this chapter's interview. It is for love that Eve ate of the fruit of the Tree of the Knowledge of Good and Evil. Love may be the deepest motivation within a woman who embodies the feminine energy of Eve. Eve also initiated free will for humanity because of her thirst for love. Freedom and love are intertwined. There cannot be love without freedom. As much as we may want to love or be loved, love cannot be coerced.

A woman is a co-creator with the Divine. Because the woman has been endowed with a greater sensitivity, she was given the privilege of birthing new life from her body. She experiences herself naturally connected to others and to "mother" Earth.

In addition to the privilege of being a vehicle for the physical, emotional, and spiritual birth of a human being, a woman can birth a new consciousness that expresses greater connectivity for the world. It is for this reason that the woman is considered to be a more refined sensitive being. Humanity looks to the feminine for this kind of revelation of Godliness. Generally speaking, masculine energy refers to the conquering of new terrain, bestowing good, and fighting evil. Feminine energy is about revealing love and connection, and experiencing the deepest light and love in one's own body.

The design of our physical bodies also reveals an important difference between the masculine and feminine. For a man, sex takes place outside of his body, his sexual organ becomes rigid, tension builds, and he must enter and penetrate another body to experience sexual intimacy. For a woman, sexual union takes place within.

A woman must open herself to receive a man and allow his penetration. Love allows her to receive a man's gifts. Her ability to trust herself and surrender to God shapes her receptivity. When a woman is most open, she is vulnerable, beautiful, and courageous.

Love, intimacy, and relationship are most important to the feminine. She should bear no shame of her innate yearning to love and be loved for this is what she teaches the world. By her very being and natural radiance, a woman lifts up the consciousness of all around her to greater love and receptivity. When a woman feels loved, and loves and nurtures others, she feels most fulfilled and alive.

What Spiritual Practice Can We Learn from Eve?
The Spiritual Practice of Holy Intimacy

Our sexuality is a powerful biological and physical urge and it connects us to the deepest and innermost core of our souls. Thus, sexuality provides us the opportunity to make the highest forms of unification. According to Rabbi Moses ben Nachman Gerondi, known as the Ramban or Nachmanides, sexual relations bring wholeness not only to us, but it radiates spiritual energy, peace, and healing to the world. Though the sexual act is brief, its effects spread to all aspects of our lives.

Sexuality is very important to a woman, possibly even more than a man. For that reason, according to Jewish law, a husband has to provide a woman with sexual relations as she desires during the appropriate times. For example, he can't leave for business trips that would minimize her times for sexual fulfillment. Unfortunately, many women are not enjoying sexual relations as much as they could. Sexual dysfunction is rampant among married couples today.

Sexual relations are even experienced as burdensome to many women. As a therapist, I found that it is unfortunately very common for women to have sexual relations as a form of obligation. Others may even refuse to have sex, preferring cuddling in place of sexual penetration.

The purpose of sexual relations is ultimately to give pleasure to the woman. The body of a woman is designed by God with the ability to receive greater pleasure and enjoyment from sexual relations than for men. Every woman must know this for herself. According to Jewish law, it is more important for man to satisfy and please his wife than himself. This unique pleasure, joy, and knowledge experienced in sexual union is what Eve wanted and why she ate of the Tree of the Knowledge of Good and Evil and gave it to Adam. The *tikkun* (healing) of the feminine asks that women give themselves permission to enjoy sexual relations.

A woman is sensitive to the fusion of love and sex. A woman's heart and genitals are more deeply connected than those of a man. In the act of sexual relations, a woman must allow herself to be penetrated as the man's sexual organ enters her innermost chambers. It is natural and necessary for her to be more discriminating and less promiscuous than a man. As such, a woman must use discernment to control the gates of what she allows to enter her and never allow a man to enter her whom she does not love nor want his energy to reside within her. Yet she must also be able to surrender and open her gates, for it is through holy sexual intimacy a woman experiences her true spiritual and physical fulfillment. Her very body is a vehicle for the greatest revelation of Godliness.

A woman who engages in promiscuous sexual relations because she is seeking validation of her femininity, male approval, love from others, or for any other external benefit, will not feel fulfilled. Her self-esteem will actually be diminished from participating in acts of sexuality that are not rooted in love and holiness. Though she may have the power to seduce men, she will not feel loved or honored by them.

If she acts and dresses to arouse the lust of men so as to gain power over them, she will ultimately be treated and discarded as a sexual object. It is also possible that a woman or even a girl may be sexually violated or exploited through no fault of her own. Such women will most likely need to do remedial therapeutic work to reclaim their natural birthright of healthy, enjoyable, and holy sexuality.

Sex in Judaism is a most holy act, a way to experience and reveal God in the world. Sexual relations done with the proper intention, as a spiritual act, as a demonstration of love and desire for unity with one's partner, creates protective angels for one's self and community. Sexual relations done improperly, during a woman's menstrual cycle, or for the wrong reasons, create negative consequences in one's soul and the world. Sex without connection to love, God, or holiness is simply an animalistic act. There is no real intimacy or healing possible in such an act. Furthermore, sexuality that is purely physical undermines whatever spirituality is present and creates *klippot*, opaque shells that disconnect us from the light of the Divine Presence.

There are three partners in the sexual relationship: a man, a woman, and God. Meditation and intention elevates the sexual act to the most holy act between a man and a woman. In Kabbalah, the bedroom is called the "holy of holies." In Kabbalistic sexual practices, the man is viewed as Ha-Kodesh Boruch Hu (the Holy One) and the woman as the Shechinah (the Divine Feminine). Through sexual relations, the greatest unification takes place. Holy sexuality requires character refinement and consciousness on the part of both the man and woman. Be mindful of your intentions when engaging in sexual relations.

MEDITATIVE PRACTICES OF EVE
Proper Eating
As the first "sin" took place through eating, a primary spiritual practice learned from Eve is to eat the right foods with proper intention. We ingest all kinds of food: recreation, movies, television, books, music, and our friends and acquaintances, and work. Everything we take into ourselves has the ability to strengthen or weaken.

It is necessary that we eat, but how and what we eat is important and affects who we are.

Be mindful and conscious of what you take into your body, your heart, and your soul. Love yourself enough to make nurturing choices. Before "eating," consider whether the food or activity will truly support your well-being. Does it connect you to the Divine? Is it loving and healing? Do you feel better afterward? Do you eat for immediate gratification?

Make an inventory of foods, friends, behaviors, and activities that truly nurture you. Seek to include them in your life on a frequent basis. Seek to reduce that which weakens. A depressed person, no matter the cause, needs more spiritual nutrition in their diet, such as prayer, meditation, and Torah study.

Keeping an accounting in a journal or diary can help one see the healing progress made through proper "eating." Increase positive spirituality by saying the blessings before and after eating.

Eating with Blessings

Because of our "fall," we need to eat physical foods rather than live solely on spiritual light. The first foods were fruits, then vegetables, and then fish and animals. As we develop spiritually, we are able to eat lighter foods and eliminate foods that do not nurture the body or soul.

When we say a blessing, we acknowledge God as the Creator and source of life, we align our will with Divine Will, and we draw down Divine light from above to below. The spark of Divine light from within the food is elevated and returned to the source of all life as it was an agent for blessing. We help Eve to complete her work by eating proper foods with blessings.

Eat "kosher" or vegetarian, particularly if you were born Jewish or choose to follow the Jewish path. Within the Bible, there is a clear definition of the foods that are good to eat—that is, foods that are spiritually easy to digest. We may not understand the reasons for the prohibitions of certain foods. We may even like the forbidden foods like pork, lobster, scallops, et cetera., so it will be a bit of an act of surrender and discipline to eat within the proscribed categories.

Know that these prohibitions are not logical, so do not try to understand them in this way. If they are forbidden, we must have the faith to accept that they will not support us spiritually.

Eat slowly, take a few breaths before you eat and during the course of the meal. Chew the food carefully. Be particularly conscious when eating animal such as meat and chicken. It is important that you have the consciousness of lifting up the holy sparks in the animal when you eat. If you are not Jewish, feel free to experiment with these blessings.

Blessings for Fruit: *Boruch Ata Adonai Eloyhenu Melech Ha'olam Boray Pre Ha Etz*

Blessings for Vegetables: *Boruch Ata Adonai, Eloyhenu, Melech, Ha'olam Boray Pre Ha Adama*

Blessings for Bread and Meals with Bread: *Boruch Atah Adonai Eloyhenu Melech Ha'olam Ha Motzei Lechem Min Ha Eretz*

KEY QUESTIONS FOR REFLECTION AND FOLLOW-UP DISCUSSION ON EVE

1. Was Eve a heroine? Was she simply tricked by the serpent, was she naive, or did she have a more noble intention, as stated in this book?
2. Has the more empowering interpretation of the story and the punishments explained in this book changed your understanding of yourself as a woman or man? If so, in what way?
3. The serpent is generally considered a symbol of evil in the West, responsible for beguiling Eve to eat the forbidden fruit. Instead of gaining Divine wisdom, Eve becomes aware of good and evil after eating from the Tree. She gives to Adam and they both feel self-conscious in a way they had not experienced before. In the East, the serpent is a symbol of wisdom. The serpent is the kundalini energy hidden at the base of the spine that rises to restore enlightenment to a person. Can you reconcile these two different interpretations? How do you understand the serpent?
4. Women have been oppressed throughout time and continue to be so even today in many places throughout the world. In some religions, this has even been justified due to the sin committed by Eve. How do you understand the oppression of women? If you are a woman, what have you personally experienced or witnessed?
5. For women, in what ways do you feel less than because you are a woman? How can you reframe the ways you criticize or belittle yourself, or other women, so that you celebrate the positive qualities of a woman? In what ways, do you feel good or privileged to be a woman?
6. What are the unique gifts that a woman and a man have? How do you celebrate and appreciate being a woman or a man?
7. How do you experience the energies of Lilith and Eve in your life? Can you be both loving and powerful? If you are meeting in a group of women and studying this book, take turns dancing out the energies of both Lilith and Eve. Lilith is the dark, powerful, sexual, seductive energy, and Eve is the powerful, loving, mothering, compassionate energy. Can you embrace both energies as a part of you? Can you be loving and soft when needed and also dark and fierce when necessary?
8. How does a couple transform sexual relations to be more holy, more of a God-knowing experience, a revelation of the Divine Presence, rather than simply a means for consensual physical or emotional gratification?

CHAPTER TWO

SARAH'S DISCERNMENT
THE STRENGTH OF INTEGRITY

Your insight and wisdom is different than a man's. It is foolish to imitate men and try to fit into their version of reality. The world is in great need of what you have to offer.

—*Sarah*

SARAH
PROPHETESS AND MOTHER OF THE JEWISH PEOPLE

Sarah, deemed to be one of the most beautiful women who ever lived, was the first mother of the Jewish people and considered a prophetess in her own right. Along with her husband Abraham, who taught the men, Sarah taught the women about the unity and oneness of God. In her time, when matriarchal societies were still prominent, Sarah was considered a priestess who taught women the secrets of embodying the Divine Presence.

Throughout her life, Sarah demonstrated that there was no separation between the mundane and the sublime. This is the wisdom of the Divine Feminine attributed to Sarah. It is said that her tent was perpetually open, her candles burned from one week to the next, and the bread she would bake would never go stale. Whether Sarah was doing mundane work such as cleaning the tent or in high spiritual meditation, Sarah was believed to be always connected to the Divine. If you were in her tent, you would feel the Divine Presence in an almost palpable way, the clouds of glory hovering above.

Sarah's tent was the prototype for subsequent holy places, such as the *Mishkon*, the tabernacle first built while the Jewish people journeyed in the desert, and the Holy Temple built by King Solomon. The same miracles associated with these holiest places were first revealed in Sarah's tent. Sarah is the only woman for whom a chapter in the Bible is named.

Even though Sarah lived in such an elevated consciousness of the Shechinah, the Divine Presence, her life was not without challenges. Because of famine, she traveled into Egypt with her husband, who requested she pretend to be his sister to ensure his safety. Only because of her own spiritual powers, Sarah left Egypt unharmed. While in Egypt, Sarah met Hagar, an Egyptian princess who would become Sarah's foremost disciple and favored maidservant.

After many years of infertility, Sarah offered Hagar to her husband so that Abraham could bear a child. At the age of ninety, when she had physically lost the capacity to bear children, through a visitation of three angels, Sarah's name was changed and she was blessed with a child, Isaac.

Sarah's birth name was *Yiscah*, which comes from the Hebrew *socar*, "to gaze." While Eve was considered beautiful, Sarah was deemed even more so. As a young woman, people would gather around Sarah to simply gaze upon her, and to have their hearts opened and filled with love and light. The name Yiscah referenced her as a prophetess, a seer who could see things through Divine inspiration.

When they married, Abraham changed her name to *Sarai,* which means "my princess," and she became a princess to her people. Their marriage indicated her willingness to join his mission to perfect the world. Later, her name was changed to remove the restrictive *my,* signifying that she was now princess to all nations. The addition of the Hebrew letter, *hay,* expanded her status and fate. Sarai could not bear a child with Abraham, but Sarah could.

After a visitation of three angels, Sarah gave birth to Isaac. It was a miraculous birth. Sarah's youth and beauty were restored to her.

When Isaac was around three years of age, Sarah ordered the departure of Hagar and Ishmael from their midst. This was against Abraham's wishes, but Abraham is told by God to "listen to her voice" and submits to Sarah's demands.

When Isaac was thirty-seven, God summoned his father to demonstrate his faith in God through his willingness to sacrifice his son, Isaac. Prior, Sarah was sent away to Hebron, seemingly uninformed of what was to take place. When Sarah received a vision of the pending death of her beloved son at the hand of her husband on Mount Moriah, her soul expired. If her son had been harmed in a natural way, that would have been devastating, she would have been heartbroken for the rest of her life, she would have sought consolation in God, trusted God's will—but by at hand of her husband, this was too much.

The Zohar, the esoteric commentary on the Bible, suggests that she offered her life in place of her son's. Her very last words might have been, "Take me and not my son."

Sarah was buried in the Cave of Machpelah, in Kiryat Arba in Hebron. Tens of thousands of women and men visit every year. This burial site was offered to Abraham as a gift by the owner, but Abraham insisted on purchasing it with a great deal of money. This forever removed any doubt as to the ownership.

In the Bible, read specifically about Sarah in Genesis 11:29, Genesis 12:14–17, Genesis 16:5, Genesis 21:9, and Genesis 23:1–2.

INTERVIEW WITH MOTHER SARAH

Mother Sarah, what is your message to women today?
Sarah: Know your worth as a woman. You are a woman, know that you are a priestess. As a woman, you hold the keys to creation within your body and your soul. Within you are the holy secrets and mysteries of life itself. You have come

into the physical world, not for your enjoyment, but to embody the holiness and light of the Shechinah, the Divine Feminine Presence.

Respect yourself and listen to what is in your heart. Your insight and wisdom is different than a man's. It is foolish to imitate men and try to fit into their version of reality. The world is in great need of what you have to offer. Women and men do not know of the power and the holiness of the feminine. For thousands of years, the path of the feminine has been diminished and hidden, but this will soon change.

You are more beautiful and precious than you can imagine. Know that there are many in the higher planes of being who are supporting you. I love you. Call on me and I will help you.

What is the feminine way to connect to God?

Sarah: The feminine path to God is simple. Programmed within your very cells is the knowledge of how to be a vessel for God. Women know how to do this, opening and receiving, but men may learn how to do this as well. A woman need not toil as much as a man for a revelation of Godliness. She only needs to open herself to whom she really is, for she is actually an expression and embodiment of the Shechinah. Men tend to make life quite complex and abstract but it need not be for women. Give yourself time to meditate, for it is there that you will discover who you really are, and what you need to do in this world. Open your heart and the Shechinah will reveal Herself to you, from within you.

Is there a spiritual practice besides meditation that I should do?

Sarah: One of the tools given to you a woman to experience the Shechinah, or those on the feminine path, both Jews or non-Jews, is to light candles for the Sabbath, holidays, or at any time at all. There is such wisdom to be received from candle-lighting when you give yourself time to receive. It is really quite simple. Through lighting candles, you are given the gift of direct access to the holy healing light of God. Meditate on the light of the candle and let it fill your being. When you are in this consciousness, you reveal the light of the Shechinah. Take the time to gaze at the candle light. Take time to reflect on what others need and send healing light to them as well. This is a very magical time for a woman.

There was always light in your tent. How was this possible?

Sarah: The light of the candles I lit was ignited and sustained by my continual awareness of God. My consciousness was drawn inward. I lived for most of my physical life on earth joyfully in a state of consciousness, of deep meditation, and of clinging to the Divine. As I tapped into the eternity of God's light, my candlelight was always lit. In this way, all who saw my tent, or beheld it from afar, would know that God is always present in this world.

Dearest child, my beloved one, the very same spiritual light that sustained my candles is also available to you. It is a gift of the Holy One that the Presence of God may be experienced and manifested in this physical world. The light of Godliness is always present if you but see through the veil of physicality.

The external world functions with the light of the sun. Life under the sun is all about doing, accomplishing, and achieving. This is what masculine energy is all about. But the light of the candle is given to the women. The light of the candle illuminates passageways to the hidden and deeper realms of being. It is here that you will find the beauty and love that you seek. The secrets of God are revealed through candlelight. Remember that the external world with all its fascination, beauty, and excitement will never offer you what you can experience through the subtle but infinite illuminations within yourself. It is for this reason that I remained most constantly in my tent.

In Judaism, women have been given the responsibility of lighting candles to initiate holidays and the Sabbath for the home. If there is no woman present, a man must do this for himself. Why is it important for women to light candles?

Sarah: By the light of a woman's consciousness, she will make her home a place of peace and love or, God forbid, one of strife and misery. The happiness and well-being of her family is a reflection of her consciousness. A woman has the privilege to reveal the spiritual light of the Shechinah to illuminate the atmosphere of her home, particularly through the lighting of candles.

Beloved one, know that your thoughts create reality. As a woman, the reality that you create is inhabited by everyone around you. Be particularly conscious what thoughts you want magnified in your life. Everything in life begins with thought. You can choose your thoughts.

If your intention is to bring light and love into your home and into the world, the highest most refined spiritual light will flow through you. The consciousness you open to when you light candles will leave a holy scent in your home, and it will be felt by all who enter. Everyone will know intuitively if God is present in your home. Remember that the more light you share with others, the more spiritual light will flow through you.

Do you have some general guidance for people, men and women alike, beginning on a spiritual path?
Sarah: It is necessary to surround yourself with God-loving, life-affirming people who will support the highest expression of who you are. If they are not that, then help them to become the kind of people they are meant to be. At the same time, you may need to separate yourself from those who will not change and seek to undermine you.

Muster the courage needed to make important lifestyle changes, to live your life according to the values that promote life rather than death. It may not be easy, but know that you always have a choice. The choices you make now will influence the conditions you will have to confront in the future. Choose life. Do not abandon your own inner knowing and your own integrity in order to take care of or please others.

If you know anything about my life, you will know that I was not a people pleaser and you need not be as well. Your life must be internally validated, solely by your conscious connection with the Shechinah. Be strong.

Mother Sarah, you traveled with your husband in the desert. What was that like for you?
Sarah: When I occupied a physical body, I lived in the consciousness of God. I was completely attuned to the Shechinah; She guided my steps. That was more than enough. I did not have to know where I was going. I experienced the holiness of each moment. I always trusted that where I was, where I went, and who I met were all a part of the Divine plan. My faith sustained me. I was never afraid. My husband had received a Divine command to leave our home and I went with him, of course.

Many people are angry to hear that your husband did not protect you when you entered Egypt. He asked you to deny your marriage to him, to say you were his sister, so he would be safe. You were kidnapped by Pharaoh. It seemed like Abraham was concerned about himself and not about you. Were you not afraid or angry?
Sarah: I was not frightened spending a night in the palace of Pharaoh and later in the palace of King Abimelech. I knew that no one can hurt me unless it was Divine Will. I also had the command of the angelic forces that would protect me and harm those who might try to hurt me. I was not angry with Abraham, for he did not know that about himself nor did he have the same abilities as I. He knew

that I would be safe. No harm would come to me. He did not trust that he would be protected in the same way that I was.

When I was in the palaces, I was treated like royalty. The Pharaoh and then later King Abimelech wanted to marry me. To make me the queen of their empires, they offered me half of their kingdom: all their wealth and luxuries beyond my wildest fantasies. I was not tempted, even though my life would be much easier than with Abraham wandering around the desert. I knew what my spiritual mission and purpose was and that I would accomplish this by being married to Abraham. No amount of riches and honor in the world would make me compromise or sell out what I came into this world to birth. I had total clarity and focus. Abraham and I came into this world to teach people about the oneness of God. Is there anything loftier or more wonderful than that?

My beloved daughters and my precious sons, remember that the physical world is a world of illusions, so be very careful. Remember what you came into this world to do. You did not come here to accumulate material possessions, so why do you give so much energy and time to them. Know your worth. Do not measure your worth by the yardstick of materialism or worldly values. Meditate always on what pleases the Shechinah and be guided internally. Maintain your focus and you will be protected and happy.

Be fruitful and multiply is one of the first and most important commandments in the Bible. Mother Sarah, would you speak a little bit about the long period of childlessness that you endured before the miracle of the birth of Isaac? Do you have any words to offer for people going through this challenge or other challenges?

Sarah: When confronting any challenge, a person needs to know that everything comes from God. Therefore, one must seek to find the good waiting to be revealed in whatever experience they are facing. Do not think too much about what you want and what you do not have, but reflect and meditate only upon how you may connect with the Shechinah through whatever is happening to you. This connection is the essence of why you are in this world.

Nevertheless, I know firsthand how sad and heartbreaking it is to not be able to bear children. My heart is with you. If this is your plight, you must always remember that there are other ways meant for you to nurture life. You do not need to have biological children to be a mother. Look around you. There are so many people and situations that can benefit from your love and wisdom. If you tune into the Holy One, your prayers will be answered. It may not be in exactly the way you wanted, but if you pray deeply enough, you will be transformed through prayer. You will be happy and rejoice in the blessings that are yours.

Why did you arrange for Hagar to have relations with your husband?

Sarah: When I became old and it was no longer biologically possible for me to bear children, I finally accepted that it was not my destiny to have a child. I then arranged for Hagar to be a surrogate mother for me. I reasoned that if the Holy One did not grant me a child, it must mean that I was to fulfill my destiny in another way. Hagar was my most beloved disciple. I loved and trusted her as I did my husband, so I arranged for her to have relations with my husband. I underestimated the impact of this experience for the two of them. I was naive. I did not expect that I would be betrayed by each of them.

From this one time of sexual relations, Hagar became pregnant. After all the kindness I had shown her, she taunted me, telling everyone that she would soon take my place as the wife of Abraham and as the matriarch of the Jewish people. She announced to all the women who would come to visit me that she was more righteous than I was because she became pregnant with my husband at the first attempt while I could not bear a child after so many years. Abraham unfortunately encouraged her with these dreadful fantasies.

She was my servant, but Abraham treated her as a wife. He might have been taken by her youth and physical beauty, but nevertheless, he did not have my permission to marry her. I of course confronted Abraham. I told him as it is recorded in the Holy Bible, "The outrage is due to you. It was I who gave my maidservant into your lap, and now that she has conceived, I became lowered in her esteem. Let Hashem judge between me and you" (Gen. 16:5).

He did not fight me. He knew that he did not have the right to liberate and marry Hagar. She was given to me when we left Egypt. Once I nipped this matter in its root with Abraham, it was necessary to make it clear to her that I would no longer be abused or humiliated by her. Hagar initially ran away but returned and bore her son Ishmael. It was not easy for me, I remained childless, but I accepted this challenge as Divine Will.

After everything I went through, the Holy One had compassion for me. My name was changed to Sarah, which means "princess for the nations," from Sarai, which means "my princess." This was a name that Abraham had given me when we were young. From the moment my name was changed, I was transformed. My youth and my beauty were restored to me. It was a great miracle. I was able to bear a child when I was ninety years old.

Mother Sarah, many people are troubled by your sending away Ishmael and Hagar. Would you please explain what that was all about?

Sarah: There are those who say that my decision to send Ishmael and Hagar away was one of jealousy. You must know that it was not. If it were jealousy, there would be nothing that you could learn from me, and the Holy One would not have told Abraham to listen to me.

What I did was hard but necessary. Abraham and I were charged with the important mission of spreading the teachings of the unity of God and safeguarding the holy transmission and revelation of YHVH for all generations. This transmission must be pure and uncontaminated by idolatry. The existence of the world depends on this purity of this transmission. It was very clear that Hagar and Ishmael would not forsake idolatry and that they would have a negative influence on Isaac. Ishmael was already indicating his desire to usurp the birthright of my son. When I witnessed him pretending to direct target practice with his bow and arrow at my beloved son, I knew that he might harm or even kill him. I feared for Isaac's physical safety.

Know that I did what I did to protect the physical safety and the sanctity of my son and all the descendants who would carry the holy transmission of YHVH (The Divine Tetragrammaton). I did what was necessary and it was confirmed by God. I am sorry and pained that so many people have had to suffer until the world wakes up to the truth.

Your decision created separation between the Jewish people and the Arabs, the descendants of Ishmael. It seems that we are still paying for that decision.

Sarah: My beloved ones, my heart is with you. I know how hard and painful these times are. You must be patient. The situation in the world will have to become more intense until it becomes better. Regarding the difficult situation between the Arabs and the Jews, I cannot and I do not take responsibility for that. I did not cause this hatred. Rather, in sending Ishmael away, I demonstrated to the Jewish people for all time what they must do to safeguard life and the integrity of the spiritual mission they have. In time the world will acknowledge the unique role that the Jewish people have played. There will be peace.

Remember the prophecy that Hagar received. "He shall be a wild-ass of a man. His hand shall be against everyone" (Gen. 16:12). Isaac was too young and not strong enough to protect himself from the influence of Ishmael. Ishmael has been blessed by Abraham, yet his descendants are jealous of the blessings of others. Too often they provoke war with others because of these jealous feelings.

You have only to look around your world to see the fulfillment of this prophecy. The jealousy of others will ultimately be the downfall of the people of Ishmael. In the end, they will learn the foolishness of jealousy. It will be the hard way, but they will learn.

Can you offer any other guidance to the Jewish people?

Sarah: There will be war between the Jewish people and the people of Ishmael over the ownership of the Land of Israel. The Jewish people have failed to claim ownership of the land according to the prophecies received by Abraham. The land is a Divine gift to my descendants and must be treasured as such. Ishmael cannot be expected to value the holiness of this transmission when the Jewish people do not.

When the Jewish people recognize that the Land of Israel is holy, that it is unique and not like other nations, the people of Ishmael will accept that as well. Then there will be peace.

Everyone talks about the greatness of Abraham's willingness to sacrifice Isaac, and Isaac's (Yitzchak) willingness to surrender his life, but little is said of the impact on you.

Sarah: I was totally devastated when I saw in a vision that my husband was going to kill my precious and only son. My son was my life. In a single moment's time, my whole life with Abraham seemed like a total sham. This act was against everything I valued in life.

The death of my son by the hand of my husband was more than I could bear. So many thoughts and feelings rushed into my head. Why did Abraham not consider what this act would mean to me? How could he be so selfish? Was he unconsciously paying me back for me sending Ishmael away? God had told him before to listen to me. Why did he not consult me before planning to do this horrific act?

You died alone, abandoned, and betrayed by your husband and your son.

Sarah: Do not worry or be pained on my account. It is true that I was deeply pained for a few moments, but then I knew that I needed to act quickly to save my son. I consciously chose to intercede before the throne of mercy for the life of my son. I was in the company of my handmaidens, holy women I lived with for many years, when I left my physical body.

Let me die. Let me be the sacrifice, and not him. **Take me and not my precious son.**

My prayer was answered. My son lived and I left the physical world. Ask any mother. She would have done what I did.

It was clear to me that after saving my son's life, my work in the physical world was complete. I knew my son and his soon-to-be wife would assume the mantle and continue the holy work that Abraham and I began. I would continue to guide him from the other side. There was nothing more that I needed to do in life, but something very important that I needed to demonstrate through my death.

From my death, let it be known that there are things in life worth dying for.

What more can we learn from your death?

Sarah: Please know that I value life. I could not live in a world where life was not valued. My husband, and men throughout time, seem to need to prove themselves through acts of bloodshed and violence. That is not the path of the feminine that I taught and want to impart to you. The feminine path is all about loving life, revealing Godliness, and even experiencing the holiness of God in one's body.

With my death, sadly enough, a new order began for women and men. Women would no longer work in the forefront as I did, but would have to work more behind the scenes, in supportive roles. Not for a long time would the prophecy of the woman be as honored as was mine.

The situation is still similar today. Men still engage in war. Do you have any final words for women and men today?

Sarah: You live in awesome and awe-inspiring times. Now is the time to reclaim the path of the feminine that I began. You will be supported from on high by many great ones. Doors to palaces of spiritual delight that have been closed for so long will now easily open for you to enter, but you must stay clear and focused. Know your worth. Keep yourself pure. Love life. Be strong.

May you be privileged to lift the veil of the Shechinah so Her light may shine throughout the world. May the peace of Her revelation come soon and easily to Israel and the entire world. Thank you for all your good work, my beloved sons and daughters. I support you. I love you.

CALLING OUT TO MOTHER SARAH

(It is suggested that this be read out loud by the reader or the group)

> *Mother Sarah, we bear witness to your pain. You did not die in vain. Your pain is our pain. We hear a strong message of the value of life in your death.*

We understand that you could not remain in such a world that your son would be sacrificed. Mother Sarah, we are your children. We honor your voice, your power, and your life. In your lifetime, you were the embodiment of the Shechinah, the Divine Feminine. With your death, the voice of the Divine Feminine became more hidden.

We have learned so much about the path of the feminine from your teachings and example. Help us to have the courage and integrity to speak and live our truth like you did. So many of us are looking for our voice, we have been silenced. We do not speak our truth. Too often we avoid conflict and seek to please others rather than assert our truth. Help us to be fearless like you.

In reclaiming the path of the feminine, we promise to value the fullness of life as it is. We will value ourselves and each other above the abstract idealization of life. This is our pledge to you, our spiritual mother. With our love and our discernment, we will redeem the Shechinah from Her hiding. With the blessings of the Holy One and you, we will indeed lift the veil that is covering Her and let Her light shine in all Her splendor.

PRAYER TO THE GOD OF MOTHER SARAH

May the God of Mother Sarah guide me to make the choices that serve my highest good. May the God of Mother Sarah empower me with the strength to remain true to my vision even though it may not be what others would want of me.

What Quality of the Feminine Does Sarah Demonstrate?

Sarah models a woman who can stand her ground doing what she feels necessary, even if it is not popular or is against the wishes of her husband. The Kabbalah, the esoteric wisdom within Judaism, states that a higher level of intuition and inner strength lies within a woman. She must employ these qualities in her life for the betterment of the world.

This is contrary to Western concepts of femininity as soft and helpless. Kabbalah describes feminine energy as analytical enough to make distinctions and strong enough to set necessary boundaries. It is the power of the feminine to discern what needs to be included and assimilated from that which needs to be separated and released from one's contact.

SARAH'S DISCERNMENT

Not too long after the birth of Isaac, Sarah ordered that Hagar and Ishmael be sent away. This command distressed Abraham. After all, Ishmael was his son. Sending away Ishmael was against everything that Abraham believed in. The spirit of Abraham was universal, embracing, and inclusive. Blinded by his kindness, he could not see what was happening in his own house.

How could he send away his son? God told him to listen to and obey Sarah. It is Abraham who surrenders himself, his thoughts and his feelings to the voice of Sarah. He is told to obey her even if he disagrees with her. Her insight is deeper than his. Sarah was focused and strong. She did not waiver in this order despite the pain it would cause her husband.

The Torah says "listen to her voice," not "listen to her words" (Gen. 21:12). The voice better reflects the inner essence of a person. The Zohar says the Torah wanted to emphasize that Sarah was on a higher prophetic level than Abraham. It was not necessary that Abraham understand what she said, only that he surrender to her wisdom.

Masculine energy is generally not endowed with the same capacity for discernment as the feminine. Too often a woman defers to a man when she knows better. A woman is generally yielding, flexible, and loving, yet she must also exercise discernment and listen to her own inner knowing. It may be necessary, however, for her to purify and distill her intuition so that it is heart-based and free of egoism and selfishness.

We learn from Sarah's example that a woman must find the inner strength to honor her own inner knowing. Many women suffer from low self-esteem when they deny their own truth in order to meet the needs and wishes of others and/or to avoid conflict. They may like to pretend to themselves and others that this behavior is selfless, but it is not. When we do not feel good about ourselves, we often seek validation from others, even at the expense of our own truth. This is a common tendency for many women, but is also prevalent with men who have learned that they also need to give themselves up to be loved.

When we continue to betray ourselves and what we know as our truth to please others, to be loved and validated by others, our self-esteem is further diminished. We lose connection with our soul. If we find we are overly concerned with what others think of us, we need to remember Sarah. We should step back, and engage in self-inquiry to reclaim our own knowing and self-worth.

Make an assessment in your life to determine if there are people, activities, and behaviors in which you engage that do not support you in going forward to be the person you want to be. Exercise discernment. You can let go of what does not serve you or the revelation of God in the world.

If it does not seem possible to do this yourself, seek help from friends, clergy, or a therapist. Do not be a people pleaser. Do not give up your inner truth.

What Spiritual Practice Can We Learn from Sarah?
The spiritual practice of candle lighting.
"Her candles burned the entire week."

Light candles on the Sabbath, for holidays, and any time you want to become closer to God. Meditate prior to lighting candles. Let go of concerns of the day. If you are feeling any anger or resentment, let it go. You must let it go. Try to make amends with anyone with whom you are harboring anger, or with anyone who may be angry with you. Forgive everyone. The very act of forgiveness will open you to receive. Know that you only hurt yourself by being angry. Your anger keeps you small, closed, and not able to receive God's gifts.

As you stand before the candles, pray for the ability to be a channel for the light of God's Presence.

Light a candle for every person in your home, including yourself, and take time to reflect upon the unique light of every member of your family. Meditate and send light to each person for whom you light a candle. Open your heart and be filled with love and compassion for everyone. As you gaze at the light, pray that your eyes be purified, so you see what is really important for you, your family, and your friends.

You can also see what others need to shine more brightly in their lives as well. Trust that what comes into your consciousness is a message. It is an auspicious time for you to send healing blessings to those in need. Visualize each person as a candle, shining brightly. You have a responsibility to share the light with others. Teach other women how to light candles.

If you are a married woman, keep the following thought in your mind and deep in your heart: your husband and children are in need of the light of God that only you can reveal and radiate. There is much that you receive from your husband, but when you light candles you can give to him what he really needs. You can help him to access his soul. If possible, ask him to stand next to you when you light candles and say "Amen" to your blessing. It is no accident that you are married to this man. You are here to uplift him and help him fulfill his life purpose. When he witnesses you lighting candles, he will honor you as the priestess of the home, and of his soul.

What Meditative Practice Can We Learn from Sarah?
Meditation for Divine protection

Sarah was protected by God in the house of Pharaoh and later with King Abimelech.

When you experience yourself fearful, repeat the following affirmation in meditation:

SARAH'S DISCERNMENT

I am protected by the Divine Presence. God is within me and surrounds me.
I am protected by the Divine Presence.

Take a few breaths. As you inhale, the body opens. As you exhale, you release tension. With each breath, visualize yourself becoming a vessel. Allow yourself to feel empty. Let go of passing thoughts. Open to the joy of being an empty vessel. Visualize luminous white light entering through the top of your head flowing through the body. Let this light surround you and enter into your body temple. Imagine that you can embody the Divine Presence as Sarah did.

KEY QUESTIONS FOR REFLECTION AND FOLLOW-UP DISCUSSION ON SARAH

1. Do you think that Sarah should have waited to be blessed with a child of her own, trusting in the prophecy her husband received without volunteering Hagar to be a surrogate mother? Or was it necessary for her to take the action that she did. What would you have done in Sarah's situation and why? Would you have waited or taken an action like she did?
2. Rabbinic commentaries inform us that Abraham was quick to accept Sarah's proposal. How do you imagine Sarah might have felt by his eagerness? Understandably, the request had to come from Sarah, but why was he so eager to have sexual relations with Hagar? Do you think that Abraham caused the rift between the women? Why is there no recorded prayer request for a child as with the other matriarchs and patriarchs?
3. Did Sarah have a choice to not send Ishmael and Hagar away, considering the danger that Ishmael posed to Isaac? Was it the right choice to send them away? Whether you agree with Sarah's decision or not, was Sarah modeling what to do with evil people in our midst who seek to destroy us?
4. Notice that the Bible does not record Sarah bribing, placating, or pacifying the kind of behavior demonstrated by Ishmael. Why not? What do you think?
5. Sarah's approach may not be seen to be "politically correct" in our time, but is it relevant to us today?
6. Can we heal the rift between Sarah and Hagar today by making peace between their descendants? How do we make peace?
7. Several rabbis say that Sarah committed suicide when she asked God to judge between herself and Abraham in the sending of Hagar and

Ishmael away. Does this interpretation resonate with you? Did she simply die of grief or old age? Was it suicide to offer her life as a replacement for her son?
8. There are rabbinic interpretations that say that Sarah died of joy knowing that her son was going to be sacrificed or disappointment that he wasn't? What do you think? What do you think of Sarah's closing statements in this book about why she died?
9. What challenges do you have in your life for which Sarah is a model? Take time to write about this or share it with another person.
10. What do you want to say to Mother Sarah? If you could talk with her, what would you say to her?

CHAPTER THREE

REBECCA'S HIGHER TRUTH
THE ART OF SPIRITUAL DECEPTION

A woman is inherently more attuned to what is hidden, inner, and holy, and is guided to reveal and actualize this dimension of reality when necessary by whatever means that are available to her.

—*Mother Rebecca*

REBECCA
PROPHETESS AND MOTHER OF THE JEWISH PEOPLE

There is a little-known tradition that a righteous person is not taken from this world until a successor has been born. The Bible records Rebecca's birth prior to mentioning Sarah's death, even though Rebecca was born after Sarah died. Rebecca, the second matriarch of the Jewish people and the wife of Isaac, was the daughter of Bethuel, the nephew of Abraham, and the granddaughter of Milcah, sister of Sarah.

After the death of his wife Sarah, Abraham sent his most trusted disciple Eliezer to look for a wife for his son Isaac. He sent him to his birthplace, the land of Aram. The Bible records in great detail Eliezer's scheme and the events around this search for the woman worthy of being the wife of Isaac and the matriarch for the Jewish people.

When Rebecca offered water to Eliezer and to his camels, she fulfilled Eliezer's pre-planned criteria. In acknowledging the miraculous nature of this encounter, Rebecca and her family gave their consent for her to leave her home and marry Isaac, a considerably older man.

Rebecca is often referred to as a "rose among thorns," a beautiful metaphor in Song of Songs to describe Israel among the nations. As a child, Rebecca was surrounded by negativity, duplicity, and evil, but she herself remained pure. The Bible tells us that Isaac found comfort after Sarah's death only after he married Rebecca. The miraculous signs that were associated with Sarah were once again restored when Rebecca entered the tent of Sarah.

When Rebecca had been barren for twenty years, Isaac prayed profoundly for a child with Rebecca. His prayers were answered when Rebecca became pregnant with twins. Rebecca was unsure about what was occurring within her. The children agitated within her and she said, "If so, why am I thus?"

She consulted Shem, the prophet of the time, to understand what was happening within her. "Two nations are in your womb, two regimes from your insides shall be separated, the might shall pass from one regime to the other, and the elder shall serve the younger" (Gen. 25:23).

When Isaac was old and wanted to bless his sons, Rebecca overheard her husband's plan and quickly schemed a way to deceive him and secure the blessing for her son Jacob. Jacob was initially reluctant to participate in this ruse, but

Rebecca assured him that she would protect him. The final biblical comments about Rebecca include her instructions to Jacob to seek shelter with her brother Laban and find a wife for himself there.

Rebecca's prophecy of "the elder will serve the younger" (Gen. 25:23) has important implications for future times. What this means is that the Christian nations, considered a code for Esau in the world, will in time seek their fulfillment and protection through their alignment with Israel. In the "End of Days," Israel and the Jewish people will be seen as a blessing to the world.

The global Christian community in large part has shown a growing sense of gratitude to the Jewish people for providing the essentials of their faith. Israel's best friends are found in the Christian evangelical community of America. Not only do they give millions of dollars each year to Israel, they visit Israel on spiritual pilgrimages in even greater numbers than Jews.

This can be seen as a belief that the blessings of America may be attributed to a pro-Israel policy as stated in the prophecy given to Abraham. "I will bless those who bless you and he who curses you, I will curse" (Gen. 12:3). It is therefore in America's best interests that America support Israel. The idea of being a fair broker between the Arabs and the Jews in settling the Middle-East conflict is fortunately not one that is embraced by evangelical Christians. Until Christian Zionism becomes more prominent, the ongoing battle between Christian nations and Israel represented by Esau and Jacob will continue under the banner of anti-Zionism.

Rebecca's prophecy reminds us at times of despair that there will be an end to this conflict, a time of peace.

For more information about Rebecca, read excerpts in Genesis 22:23 to 27:42–46.

INTERVIEW WITH MOTHER REBECCA

What is your message for people today?

Rebecca: In "the End of Days" there will be peace. Truth will be clear and all that is not true will be clearly seen. Be patient. Life has never been easy, but one must have faith and know that it will be good in the end. There will be peace and prosperity.

Thank you for this powerful encouragement. We live in a time of much war and corruption. Our world sometimes seems hopeless and frightening. How did you acquire this faith and perspective?

Rebecca: I was born into a home and place where hypocrisy, duplicity, and lies were everywhere. I knew intuitively at an early age that I would have to find the truth within myself. In that way, I would be safe and protected. I did not want to be like the people around me. Most people around me would say one thing but do another. They would try to appear to be good, but it was easy for me to see that they were not who or what they appeared to be.

Most people in my family and my town were selfish, always calculating what they would receive from others, by whatever means necessary. They always had ulterior motives when they did something good. I was less complicated. I knew early on that the greatest joy in life was to serve other people. It was that simple. When I was giving to others, I was happy and I felt safe. I therefore always looked for ways that I could help other people.

Is that why you gave the water to Eliezer and his camels? That is the first story about you in the Bible.
Rebecca: Yes, exactly. Eliezer, Abraham's servant, was a strong man. He could easily have gotten water for himself and his camels. But, before he could get the water for himself, I quickly rushed to offer it as soon as I saw him come near the well. I let him drink to his satiation, and then I fetched water for his camels.

I was happy when he allowed me to give to him in this way. He was clearly a stranger in our town. I knew in my heart what a great honor it is to welcome a stranger into your community. And you see how I was rewarded. I was selected to marry such a holy person, Isaac, and I could also leave my family and town as well. What a privilege! What a gift! God is so good.

You married Isaac when you were young. Please describe your life with him.
Rebecca: Being married to Isaac was a great blessing for me. I was able to grow spiritually in ways that I could not have imagined. We were close and happy with each other. Even though there was a considerable age difference between us and we came from different backgrounds, we loved and respected each other. I was his only wife, unlike the other patriarchs who married more than one woman.

If you were so close with him, why didn't you tell him of the prophecy you received when you were pregnant? Why did you go to Shem and not to him?
Rebecca: I must admit that I was embarrassed by the discomfort I had during my pregnancy. I was afraid that it was because I was unworthy of Isaac. Something must have been wrong with me because of my family background. If I were truly a righteous woman, I would not suffer so. I felt it was best to seek counsel from someone other than my husband. By going to someone objective, I could then

receive guidance on how I could improve myself and not be diminished in the eyes of my husband.

When you found out the reason and meaning of what was happening to you, why then didn't you tell Isaac? He was your husband and these were his children. It would seem he should know.

Rebecca: The main reason that I didn't confide in Isaac later was that I didn't want to embarrass or disturb him. My husband Isaac was, after all, the greatest prophet. His holiness and his level of prophecy were much greater than that of Shem and Eber. I had to assume that if he was supposed to know this prophecy, he would have known.

There must be a reason why God did not reveal this matter to him. Please know that it was not easy for me to keep this secret for all those years, but I did so to honor as well as protect my Isaac.

Why did Isaac need your protection?

Rebecca: My husband was so holy, so good, and so pure. He was more spiritual than he was physical. Remember how he was willing to give his physical life to God by the hand of his father without question. Prior to our marriage, he spent fourteen years in the tents of Shem and Eber, totally shielded from contact with evil or the mundane.

He rarely spoke about this event, but I know it changed him forever. He was always more connected to God than to this world.

What do you mean?

Rebecca: So many people try to be holy, to overcome their attachment to the physical. It was the opposite with Isaac. He had to make efforts to be engaged in the physical. Whenever he did engage in the physical world, it was only to bring blessing to it. His time was spent almost continually in prayer and meditation.

I, on the other hand, was more grounded, worldly, and more able to discern good from not good. I knew how to negotiate with the world and how to get things done. It was my job as his wife to protect Isaac so his connection to God would not be disturbed. His holiness should not and would not be tarnished by contact with evil or the mundane. Because Isaac was so holy, he saw only good. He could not even see the wickedness that was in his son Esau.

It was not my place to tell him that his son was morally deficient. Esau treated his father with respect and pretended to be righteous in front of him, but the way Esau actually lived his life was quite contrary to the ways of my husband.

I easily saw through Esau's pretenses because I'd seen this kind of hypocrisy in my early childhood.

Didn't you love both your sons? It seems like you favored Jacob and didn't love Esau.
Rebecca: Isaac and I loved both our sons equally. It was not because I loved Esau less that I wanted Jacob to have his blessing.

The blessing of the firstborn would not have been good for Esau. It would have made his life worse. He wasn't capable of working together and sharing power with his brother Jacob. And with this blessing Esau would have also been in a position to cause greater harm to the world.

Though the blessing of the firstborn offered many privileges, this blessing also required much responsibility and self-sacrifice. Esau showed no evidence of any willingness to forsake the path of idolatry, murder, thievery, and everything else that he did that was in opposition to the values and ideals of my holy husband. Esau continually demonstrated that the material physical world was most important to him.

Remember, Esau had sold his birthright for a pot of lentils. It was clear that he didn't care to be engaged in the struggle necessary to transform the world into a Godly place.

Jacob was better suited for the work that needed to be done. I knew life would be hard for him, more challenging having received the blessing intended for Esau as well as the one for himself. I also knew and trusted that this blessing would force him to grow in ways that would be good for him and in ways that would bring blessing to the entire world.

Because of the prophecy I received during my pregnancy, I felt it necessary to do whatever was needed to actualize what had been revealed to me. Jacob was the younger son so I knew that he had to receive the blessing of the firstborn to fulfill the prophecy I received.

Is that why you encouraged Jacob to lie to his father? It would appear that he was initially reluctant to do so.
Rebecca: Yes. Jacob was so pure and good. He didn't want to lie to his father, but also feared the negative consequences of doing so. Perhaps he would be cursed rather than blessed. To persuade him to follow my instructions, I informed him of the prophecy I received when I was pregnant and assured him that I would protect him of negative consequences from his father Isaac. He listened and honored my request.

Was Isaac upset by the deception?

Rebecca: Initially, yes. He was upset and startled. In a very short time, however, he realized that what happened was what was supposed to happen. He came to understand that I was behind the entire deception. Because he trusted me, he then trusted that this was the right way.

If he had not believed that this was a good thing to do, he would have—and he could have—nullified the blessing. He didn't. He understood that Jacob's descendants would need the protection of this blessing.

Do you think that it was right to deceive your husband? Is it good to lie?

Rebecca: I believe it was right to deceive my husband in this particular situation. The world is based on truth, so in most instances it is important to be truthful. Honesty is the basis of trust and integrity.

Nevertheless, there are extraordinary times like what I confronted when it is good to lie, even necessary to lie. To tell the truth in such circumstances is foolish.

So when is it good to lie?

Rebecca: You need to be cunning when confronting evil. To fight evil one may even be deceitful. If Esau had been prepared to be a worthy partner in continuing the transmission of YHVH (code for the Divine Name), there wouldn't have been a need to take it away from him. But he was not, so rather than fight him directly, it was best to take the blessing away through deceit.

There is such a thing as holy lying. There is a difference between holy lying and ordinary lying. In holy lying, it is clear, after the deception, that it is the way it was supposed to be and that the outcome could not have been achieved another way. When the blessing is not revealed to a person or nation directly, one must go through the back door to receive it. That is what I did.

It was necessary I do this to actualize the prophecy I received when they were both in the womb. Because this was a most holy matter of great importance, it had to be done through deception. The more refined and higher the light and blessing, the more it is hidden, and the more deception may be necessary to reveal it. That may seem counterintuitive, but that is how it is in matters of holiness.

One way to distinguish ordinary lying or deceit is if the purpose of the lying is noble. If it was only self-serving and a person who engages in such acts loses dignity and connection to the Divine, that is ordinary lying. That did not happen to me or Jacob at all. My purpose and that of Jacob was noble.

If you look at biblical stories, women seem to engage in deception more than men. Why is that?
Rebecca: Yes, this is true. Women have a long lineage of holy lying and deception. A woman is inherently more attuned to what is hidden, inner, and holy, and is guided to reveal or actualize this dimension of reality when necessary by whatever means available. There are many examples of women throughout history engaging in deception for holy and noble purposes. Look at Tamar, who disguised herself as a prostitute to fulfill her prophecy; Judith, who disguised herself as a prostitute to seduce and murder the Greek general Holofernes. Rather than be criticized for doing what they did, they are honored. Similarly, I was not criticized for my actions. Many understand that my actions safeguarded the continuity of the Jewish people.

In retrospect, do you have regrets in this regard for your actions?
Rebecca: I do not have regrets. I did what was necessary. If Esau had received the blessing of the firstborn, he would have been in a position to do more damage to the world than he'd already done. In my mind, there was no other choice than to do what I did.

Was the blessing good for Jacob? Jacob's life was not easy. Was it even more difficult because of his stealing Esau's blessing? Furthermore, the Jewish people, the descendants of Jacob, have been persecuted and murdered by the Christian nations, the descendants of Esau, for thousands of years. It seems like the struggle continues even to modern times. Was it worth it, after all?
Rebecca: Of course it was worth it!

It is true Jacob's life wasn't easy, but his usurping this blessing was necessary to safeguard the sanctity and survival of the world. The Jewish people, the descendants of Jacob, have consequently had to carry an additional burden, requiring that they also demonstrate an enormous sacrifice. Until my son Esau and his descendants realize and accept that they must be subordinate to Jacob and his descendants and to the Creator of the world who has a special covenant with the Jewish people, there will not be peace. Be patient. In time they will.

What does this really mean? Please explain your prophecy: "The older one will serve the younger one."
Rebecca: Please know that the fulfillment of my prophecy does not mean that the Jewish people will rule the world and laud their power over the other

nations of the world. This is what the Christian-based nations of Esau have done throughout time. Jacob and his descendants are not interested in dominating the nations of the world. They are only interested in serving the Holy One and in sharing their knowledge and blessings with others so as to transform this world into a place of Godliness.

How will this happen?

Rebecca: When the spiritual principles of faith, morality, and the belief in the oneness and unity of God that are at the core of the transmission of the Jewish people are accepted by the Christian nations, then and only then will there be peace and prosperity for all. This process of the acceptance of the principles of Judaism throughout the world has already begun. There is such a thing as democracy, due to Judaism. Christians are beginning to appreciate the Jewish roots of their faith as well.

Still, anti-Semitism is rampant in our modern time. What will it take for the Christian nations to not persecute the Jewish people? Sixty years ago they wanted to annihilate the Jewish people. Now they want to destroy the State of Israel as a Jewish state. They even blame Israel for Islamic terrorism taking place throughout the world.

Rebecca: The power and protection of the Jewish people lies with their acceptance of and alignment with the covenantal relationship with God. When they seek the favor of the nations over that of God, they diminish themselves, they suffer and lose Divine blessing. When the Jewish people align themselves with God, even non-Jews seek to support them as well.

Do you have any concluding words for our readers?

Rebecca: Do not fret. Do not worry. The descendants of Esau will eventually realize the futility of war and domination and know that scapegoating and demonizing the Jewish people for their own moral failings does not help them but actually weakens them.

In time, they will appreciate all the gifts and blessings that the descendants of Jacob have bestowed upon them and the entire world. They will even be grateful that they have received so many of the benefits and blessings without having to suffer and sacrifice in the same way that the Jewish people suffered to give them. There will come a time when Christians, the descendants of Esau, will ask for forgiveness from the Jewish people. And the Jewish people will forgive because they are a compassionate loving people.

CALLING OUT TO MOTHER REBECCA
(It is suggested that this be read out loud by the reader or group.)

Mother Rebecca, you are such an inspiration to us. May your example guide us to give to others with the kind of generosity you demonstrated throughout your life. May we know directly that through giving we receive all that we need. You saw clearly at a very young age what was true and good and you were not afraid to act upon your own inner knowing. Courageously, you chose to leave all that you knew to go forward in life. You trusted your prophecy. It would have been easier for you to dismiss it, and not act upon it. You were even willing to deceive your husband and son, and absorb all the possible negative consequences because of it as well.

Help us to have your courage to trust ourselves and do whatever is necessary to actualize what we know as true in our hearts and souls. May we center ourselves in the truth that lies within the depths of our hearts so that we too live courageously. May we also be willing to go forward to make the changes we need to live more authentically. Like you did in your lifetime, may we each be willing to stand up to evil, to falsehood without fear, so we may do our part to pave a larger path for the light of the Shechinah, the Divine Presence, to be revealed in our midst. Thank you again for your courage. We love you.

PRAYER TO THE GOD OF MOTHER REBECCA

May the God of Rebecca guide me to discern what is true from what is false, what is good from what is evil, and empower me to live in accordance with my inner truth. Mother Rebecca lived in accordance with her inner truth, and so can I.

What Quality of the Feminine Does Rebecca Demonstrate?
Rebecca demonstrates all the beautiful feminine qualities exhibited by Eve and Sarah. This is understandable because Rebecca is considered a reincarnation of Sarah, and Sarah was considered a reincarnation of Eve. Rebecca's commitment to her integrity, her courage, and her willingness for self-sacrifice is perhaps more remarkable because Rebecca was born in a place where duplicity, selfishness, and

cowardice were so pervasive. Like Sarah, Rebecca demonstrates the ability of the feminine to remain true to her inner core regardless of what is happening around her. A woman in touch with her feminine essence is naturally more intuitive and should allow herself to be guided more by what is internal, that which is found within her own heart and wisdom, than by what is external.

Rebecca demonstrates so many qualities of the feminine that it is difficult to highlight only one. Surely, Rebecca demonstrates courage and faith when she leaves her parents at an early age to marry an older man she didn't know. She demonstrates the feminine quality of selfless giving when she gives water to the camels of Eliezer.

However, when she takes the steps to actualize her prophetic vision, her willingness to engage in deception to accomplish what was necessary and even to sacrifice herself in this mission, this is what truly earns her the title of mother of the Community of Israel. Jacob is frightened initially to engage in deception. Rebecca then tells him, "Let any curse be on me, my son" (Gen. 27:13). In this instance and many other times in her life, she models to all the willingness to take risks, and if necessary sacrifice oneself, for the welfare of the Jewish people and the world. The love of a mother can know no bounds.

What Spiritual Practice Can We Learn from Sarah?
The Spiritual Practice of Selfless Giving

Rebecca demonstrates abundant selfless giving in seeking water for Eliezer and his camels. It would have been generous for a young girl to provide water for the man but for the camels as well was an even greater display of giving. Furthermore, she did this on her own initiative and did not seek a reward for her action.

Selfless giving and charity are the gates to blessing and repentance. Consider several ways and projects through which you can pour unconditional abundant giving onto others. Pray and be mindful to give in as selfless a way as possible, so you are not considering what you would receive. If possible, keep this act anonymous.

If it is helpful and supportive, discuss with others the importance and benefits of selfless giving as well as the different kinds of giving. Review the kinds of giving in your life currently and how you can purify yourself through giving in a more selfless way.

KEY QUESTIONS FOR REFLECTION AND FOLLOW-UP DISCUSSION ON REBECCA

1. Do you think that Rebecca was right in not revealing her prophecy to Isaac and in encouraging Jacob to lie and steal the blessing? Did

this demonstrate a lack of faith on her part? Or rather, did she take the actions that were necessary to demonstrate faith in her personal prophecy?
2. Have there been times in your life where you have been guided to take an action reflective of a higher vision that was not savory or true on a more superficial or external level? Was this action justifiable? How did you justify the action that you took?
3. What do you think about lying and deception for holy purposes? Have you ever engaged in holy lying, saying words that are not true but served a noble purpose?

CHAPTER FOUR

RACHEL, LEAH, BILHA, AND ZILPA
WIVES OF JACOB AND HOLY MOTHERS OF THE JEWISH PEOPLE

The Power of Holy Tears To Change Oneself and the World

A woman's heart typically is more sensitive than a man's so she is inclined to cry more easily and frequently. A woman should not be embarrassed for the tears that she authentically sheds... The tears of a woman must be honored and treasured rather than ridiculed or mocked. The tears of a woman have the awesome power to arouse a blessing of Divine love and compassion and water the seeds for a fuller expression of beauty and balance in the world.. A woman's tears can penetrate the heart of God and bring down blessings to the world. When women cry, they change reality.

RACHEL, LEAH, BILHA, AND ZILPA

Rachel and Leah, the daughters of Laban (along with their lesser-known handmaidens, Bilha and Zilpa) were the wives of Jacob and the mothers of the twelve tribes of Israel. Rachel and Leah are important as archetypes of the Shechinah in Judaism. Both women are continually held in the meditation and prayers of Kabbalists who seek to reveal and foster connection between the two. I personally know Kabbalists who, in the middle of the night, wear burlap, lie on the floor, and cry for the healing of Rachel and Leah. Why would they do this?

The first meeting recorded in the Bible between Jacob and Rachel, the beautiful, selfless, and beloved one, began with a kiss. Jacob moved the rock over the mouth of the well, watered the sheep of Laban, his mother's brother, then kissed Rachel and wept (Gen. 29:10–12). It is taught that he wept because he knew prophetically that he would not be buried next to her. The Bible later tells us that he loved Rachel so much that he worked for her for seven years. Time flew by so quickly that it felt to him as if only a few days had passed.

Wouldn't waiting seven years to marry one's beloved be challenging? The Tanya, the masterpiece by Rabbi Schneur Zalman of Liadi, describes this more familiar kind of love, based on need and desire, as "love like flaming coals." Jacob's love for Rachel was a different kind of love, based on the sheer delight in the very existence of the beloved. In the Tanya this love is called "love of delights," so even waiting to marry her was a joy.

Rachel had a slightly older twin sister, Leah. Leah was intended to marry Esau, who was Jacob's older twin. While Rachel was said to be beautiful in form, Leah in the Bible is known for her "tender" eyes. When Leah heard that Esau was a wicked person, she prayed and cried that she not be forced to marry Esau. This marriage between cousins had been planned by Rebecca and Laban who were brother and sister.

Leah's prayers were answered. Her father Laban switched her for Rachel and forced her to stand in place of Rachel under the wedding chuppah (canopy). So as to not embarrass her, Rachel lovingly and selflessly gave her sister the secret signs that she and Jacob had agreed upon in the event that a possible switch would take place. It was so important to Leah to marry Jacob that she was willing to marry him even through deceit. Only in the morning after the wedding, after sexual relations had taken place, was Leah's true identity revealed to Jacob. By that time, she was already pregnant with her first son.

Leah was blessed to birth many children easily. When her first son was born, she named him Reuven and said, "God has 'seen' my affliction and now my husband will love me."(Gen. 29:32) Reuven comes from the verb "to see." When she birthed her second son, she said, "God has heard that I am the hated one, and he has therefore given me this one," and she called him Simeon.(Gen. 29:33) Simeon comes from the verb "to hear." When Leah birthed her third son, she named him Levi and she said, "This time my husband will become attached to me, for I have born him three sons" (Gen. 29:34). The selection of these names shows how important it was for her to receive Jacob's love. With each child, she prayed that her husband would love her. When Leah finally birthed her fourth son, she named him Yehudah and said, "This time I thank God" (Gen. 29:35).

With the birth of Yehudah, Leah finally felt secure in her purpose, which was to build the nation and grow in her relationship with God. She no longer expressed her anguish and her hope for her husband's love as she had previously done in the naming of her sons. Yehudah symbolized her gratitude and love of God, and was thus destined to become the leader of the Jewish people. Leah is credited as the first person in the Bible who expressed gratitude to Hashem (God). Leah is all about praising God and elevating up everything to the highest. In comparison to Rachel, who was surely Jacob's beloved, Leah felt "hated," never receiving the love of her husband for which she yearned.

Quite different than the gentle, sweet, and modest Rachel, Leah was assertive, sexual, intellectual, and willing to challenge Jacob. Leah even purchased a night with Jacob and went out to greet him with the words, "It is to me that you must come for I have clearly hired you with my son's dudaim (fertility herbs). So he lay with her that night" (Gen. 30:16). Even though Leah birthed the majority of the tribes, Jacob never moved into her tent, even after the death of Rachel.

Because building the nation of Israel was so prominent in the consciousness of both Leah and Rachel, it is important to emphasize that both women, in periods of infertility, were willing to share their husband with their handmaidens, Bilha and Zilpa. Pained by her own infertility, Rachel suggested that Jacob have sexual relations with Bilha when she finally accepted that she could not have children of her own. Leah saw the tremendous blessing occurring through Rachel's surrogacy with Bilha and decided to give her handmaiden Zilpa to Jacob in a similar fashion.

For more information about these women, read about them in Genesis 29:6 to Genesis 35:19.

INTERVIEW WITH THE FOUR MOTHERS

There are no words to describe the overwhelming honor of being in the presence of the four of you at the same time. You are the mothers of the Jewish people. What an incredible debt of gratitude we owe each of you. I would like to speak to each of you individually and then have a conversation with all of you together. May I start with Leah?

Leah, what is your message for women and men today?
Leah: I first want to convey my love and blessings to all women and men. My message to everyone is one of empowerment. Do not feel limited or resigned by what you imagine your destiny to be. If you seek to align yourself with Divine Will, you will be assisted on high.

The main thing that I want to emphasize is the importance of being focused in one's life. We each come into this world with a mission and purpose. To fulfill one's life purpose requires much effort and blessing. My life was not easy. There were many challenges and obstacles as there are in everyone's life. Yet I was able to fulfill my destiny because I was clear and focused. I not only intensely prayed, I was willing to do what was necessary to fulfill my dreams. I took great risks. And I was actually able to change my destiny.

That is my message to you. What I did you can do. You can also change your destiny.

Thank you for your inspiring and encouraging words. Is there anything more that you would like to add by way of introduction?
Leah: I also want to share with you a Divine secret that is a key to everything good in life. Besides focus and determination, be grateful for all the blessings you do have in your life. Gratitude opens the gates of blessing for a person. Every day of my life, I never forgot the kindness and love I received from my sister Rachel and my other sister wives. I named my fourth son Yehudah and he became the leader of the Jewish people. Yehudah means "I praise God, I thank God," and that I do continuously.

Would you please speak more directly about how you were able to change and fulfill your destiny?
Leah: It was my destiny to marry Esau but he was wicked. I did not want to have to be intimate with him nor bear his children. Perhaps I might have been able

to uplift and purify him, but I was not willing to make that kind of sacrifice or gamble. It was quite possible that he would have contaminated me and I would not be able to serve God in the way that I so much desired and knew that I could.

So I cried and cried. I cried for my destiny to be changed and that I be able to marry the righteous and holy Jacob. The Holy One had compassion on me as did my beautiful sister Rachel. When my father replaced Rachel with me on her wedding night and Rachel gave me the secret signs, I knew that all my tears were not in vain. It had been for this union that I prayed.

How did it feel to deceive Jacob? It seems rather unbecoming of a mother of the Jewish people to be willing to be so dishonest.

Leah: It was clear to me that this was part of the Divine plan so I was willing to do what was necessary to do my part. Jacob had "stolen" the blessings of Esau, so it was necessary that he marry me because I was the key to fulfilling those particular blessings. I told him that when he finally discovered that he had married me rather than his beloved Rachel. I said to him, "Just like you deceived your brother, so it was necessary that you be deceived. When you lied to your brother and to your father, you showed me that it is permissible to lie for a good cause. I am merely following your example."

He seemed to agree and accept my arguments. He could have divorced me after that first night when he discovered the deception, but he did not. It is true that he never divided his time equally between me and Rachel. That was very painful and challenging for me as I really wanted his love and also validation that I had indeed done the right thing by deceiving him. As time passed and I was blessed with birthing many sons, I knew in my heart of hearts that in time my husband would recognize that I was also his soul mate in addition to Rachel. God had blessed me with vision and with children so I was patient.

Will you please explain what you mean that you were blessed with vision?

Leah: It had been revealed to me prophetically that Jacob would have four wives and that there would be twelve sons who would form the Twelve Tribes. These would compose the Jewish nation. With the birth of each of my first three sons, I prayed that my husband would love me and finally acknowledge to me that our marriage was part of the Divine plan. When I gave birth to Yehudah, I experienced myself as greatly blessed, for I was given more than my fair share. This birth removed any doubt for me and confirmed to me that I had acted righteously in initially deceiving Jacob. After his birth, I knew for sure that Jacob would finally realize and accept me as his true soul mate. It became easy for me to be patient.

When I was pregnant with my seventh child, I prayed for the baby to be female, so as to not embarrass my sister Rachel. I reasoned that if I had another son, she would not be able to birth the number of tribes as even the handmaidens. She had been so kind to me that I couldn't bear her to be humiliated in that way. My prayers were answered.

The fetus within me changed to female and this child was called Dina. All in all, I was personally rewarded with six sons and one daughter, Dina, and two sons through my sister, Zilpa. I was fulfilled. I not only was blessed with such beautiful children, I experienced closeness with the Divine that healed me of any sadness or struggle I had felt previously. I finally knew in my heart that I had acted in a righteous manner, whether it was acknowledged by my husband or not.

Did you ever feel loved by Jacob?

Leah: Yes, I did. My husband was given two names, Jacob and Israel. He was named Israel after his struggle with the angel of Esau. I was the true soul mate of Israel, while Rachel was the soul mate of Jacob. He needed both time and maturity to be able to see who I was and what I offered him.

When he received his name Israel, he was finally on the level to see who I was. It was clear to each of us that we loved each other, but our love was not of this world. That knowledge made us both very joyful and fulfilled. Though he may not have lived with me when we both occupied physical bodies in your world, I am buried with Israel for eternity in the most holy burial place. I have been vindicated. I am fulfilled and deeply grateful.

Do you have a final message for people today?

Leah: I pray that my life will model to you the power of holy tears. You can change your destiny. Come to my grave, pray to me, and I will help to give you the vision and the strength to bear your burdens and transform them to blessings. I am your spiritual mother for all time.

Thank you, Leah. I would very much like to hear from Rachel now. Rachel, do you have a message for people today?

Rachel: I also begin by extending my love and blessings to everyone. Please know that I serve also as an intermediary for you. Come to my grave and cry to me and I will bring your tears to the Holy One. I am with you in your darkest moments. I will comfort you. Your prayers will be answered.

Thousands of people come each year to pray at your grave. How did your grave become one of the most special and beloved places for people to pray?
Rachel: I was buried on the road. My husband could have buried me in the family plot where I would have patiently waited for him to join me at the proper appointed time. But he was guided prophetically to bury me on the road into and out of Jerusalem, so I would be able to comfort the Jewish people when they were sent into exile from the Holy Land. I would be able to be there to greet them on the road home when they return.

Did you mind not being buried in the family plot?
Rachel: No. This was exactly what I wanted. This was the perfect place for me to reside to do the holy mothering that I always wanted to do. My exile from my proper resting place with my husband is symbolic of the exile of the Jewish people. When the Jewish people face challenges, when they are being persecuted, they come to me. I am there for the people who have not yet fully entered the Holy Land of Israel physically or spiritually.

So many people do not have the home that they want or they find themselves feeling unfulfilled in the physical world. They need the blessing of marriage, children, livelihood, peace in the home, so they come to me. A mother is always ready to be there for her children wherever they are, so it is my joy to be there for people whenever they call.

Your burial site has been the site of Molotov cocktails and other acts of terrorism in our time.
Rachel: Those who seek to destroy the Jewish people attack my grave because they know that I provide blessing to Israel. Do not fret. Their evil efforts will not be successful. My tomb will remain a center for prayer and blessing until the prophesied resurrection of the dead. This has been stated in our holy books as well.

Why was this privilege and responsibility given to you?
Rachel: I was blessed personally with two holy beautiful sons, while my sister Leah was blessed with six sons and one daughter. Being a mother was so important to me. Even though I knew it might be dangerous for me to have children, I kept trying. I died giving birth to my second son, Benjamin.

Because my heart was so overflowing with love for this beautiful holy nation and I did not have my full share of children as a full wife of Jacob, I begged

God that I be able to nurture and comfort the Jewish people even if I was not physically embodied. My prayers were answered. More than anything in this world, I wanted to be a mother to the Jewish people. Because I showed so much compassion to my sister Leah, I gave her all the secret signs so she would not be embarrassed, I continue to challenge God to be compassionate to the Jewish people. When I was flesh and blood, I reminded God that I was not jealous of my sister. So, God, why would You be jealous of idols that the Jewish people worship due to their ignorance? I have been informed that my arguments resonate with the Holy One and lessen the evil decrees cast upon them.

Why did you die so young? You were thirty-six years old when you left your physical body.
Rachel: When we were finally leaving Laban, I took my father's favorite idols on my own, without informing anyone. When my father caught up to us, he was angry and threatening. To placate my father's wrath, Jacob issued a death curse on the person who took his idols, not knowing that I was the one who committed this theft. The words of a righteous person like my husband have spiritual power.

It was not too long after this incident that I died. Because we were traveling and it was hard for me, I gave birth prematurely to my most precious son Benjamin. I named him Ben Oni, which means "son of my sorrow," but my husband changed it to Benjamin after my death.

I am stunned! I have several questions in response to what you have just stated. First, why did you steal the idols? It is a sin to worship idols.
Rachel: Everyone must know that I did not steal these idols for my personal use, but only because I wanted to weaken my father's power of sorcery. His idols were his most precious possessions. Because my father had mistreated us for so long, admittedly, I also wanted to hurt him. I wanted him to be left with nothing, and be powerless to hurt us any longer.

I was wrong not discussing this decision with my husband. At the time, I lacked sufficient trust in the God of my husband to fully protect us against my father's skilled wizardry. I kept the theft of the idols a secret because I did not want to reveal these feelings to my husband.

Did you ever forgive your husband or God for your death?
Rachel: No, not entirely, not yet. I was deeply pained to be taken away so abruptly from my beautiful children, Joseph and Benjamin, especially when they were so

young. I had prayed and shed so many tears to be granted the blessing of children. It was so sad to me that my physical life was suddenly taken from me while giving birth. The whole experience was shattering.

Because I left my physical body in childbirth, I missed all the wonderful opportunities to mother my baby, hold him, feed him, play with him, and help him and my beautiful son Joseph to grow. Tragically they were also deprived of the kind of mothering that I would have offered them. Even though I remained connected to them from my heavenly station, this was not the same as being physically present. Because of this physical separation from my children, I was then and remain eternally heartbroken.

Because of my personal heartbreak, I am deeply connected to others who are heartbroken in the physical world. Though everything that happens in life is according to the Divine plan, nevertheless, a person's pain is real. I know that personally, so I can be there for others who suffer.

Again, in answer to your question, I would have to say no, not totally, not yet. I have not totally forgiven my husband or the Holy One. When the Jewish people are redeemed from exile and the Holy Temple is rebuilt, I will forgive and rejoice with my whole heart. Until then, I will do whatever I can to awaken Divine mercy and compassion for the Jewish people through my own tears and by also being a messenger for their tears.

Do you have a message for the Jewish people?

Rachel: Come to my grave, pour out your heart, and cry to me, Mama Rachel, your spiritual mother. Please know that I was buried on the road only to let you, my beloved children, know that I am there for those who are also on the road. I am there for all those who have not yet found their place. My grave is a holy portal to the higher worlds. Your tears are holy and make a difference. Cry to the Holy One, the Creator of all.

The Jewish people have wandered through time, and they have been persecuted. It has not been fair, just as it was not fair I died so young. From my heavenly station, I want all to know with my full heart that is so filled with love for each of you that in the end the Jewish people will prevail and be victorious. Be strong and have faith. All our enemies will be destroyed or will simply vanish.

Miracles are indeed happening in your time. Look around and take note. Even though there is much strife, the Jewish people have returned to the Holy Land. More and more of the Jewish people will move to live in the Holy Land very soon. Additionally, those whose ancestors were forced to convert to other religions during this long exile from the Land of Israel will soon relinquish these shackles and return in earnest to the Jewish people. There will be more Jews living in the world than ever before. At the most auspicious time, the Jewish people will rebuild the Holy Temple on the land that had been designated to my son, Benjamin. There will be peace. Until that great day arrives, I am there for all. I will cry with you, and both guide and comfort all who come to my grave.

Thank you Rachel. There is so much more that I want to ask you, but I would like to have a few words now with the *peligishim* Bilha and Zilpa. (Peligishim are women who have sexual relations with a man without a *ketubah*, marriage contract, but with an understanding of some sort.)

Bilha, would you like to say anything to our readers? We do not know too much about you and Zilpa.
Bilha: Thank you. I have been blessed to be a handmaiden to this holy woman Rachel, to be a peligish wife to Jacob, and to be a mother to Dan and Naphtali. Though I did not name my children—Rachel named them—my children were indeed full tribes composing the nation of Israel. I am so grateful and honored to be a mother of these tribes.

Many might wonder why you agreed to be a surrogate mother for Rachel. Did you ever become jealous of her because she was the most beloved of Jacob?
Bilha: No, I loved Rachel. How could I be jealous of a person I both loved and adored! Rachel and I grew up together. Ever since I was a small child, I was given the responsibility of befriending and serving Rachel. There is nothing that I wouldn't do for her. I lived to serve her and that was enough for me.

What was your relationship with Jacob like?
Bilha: Jacob and I had a very special relationship. Because of my closeness with Rachel, he was particularly loving with me. He appreciated all that I did to help his most beloved one Rachel. We shared a deep love of Rachel and that love brought us close to each other. We also enjoyed being together, always talking about serving God and the secrets of life, but also we spoke about him, his family, and his life purpose. He was very comfortable sharing with me, probably more than any of his wives, even Rachel.

I very much wanted to be a part of this holy mission. I felt extremely blessed and honored to bear children with him. When Rachel left her physical body, Jacob moved his tent to live with me. That was natural because we spent much time together in Rachel's tent and so much enjoyed being together. I was so sad after the loss of Rachel, so his presence was such a comfort and joy to me. We helped comfort each other. We also raised Rachel's son Benjamin together. When I lived with Jacob, I experienced the Divine Presence in a way that I had not before. I was truly blessed.

Thank you. I would like to speak to Zilpa now. Would you tell us a little bit about who you are?
Zilpa: I was the maidservant of holy mother Leah. What an honor and joy to be close to her! I also was a wife to Jacob and mother to Gad and Asher. As was the case with Bilha, I also did not name my children, but they were full tribes within the House of Israel. My children added great joy to the House of Leah.

What was your relationship like with Jacob?
Zilpa: Jacob didn't spend much time at Leah's tent so I did not see him very much. That was fine with me. Leah and I used our time to cultivate and strengthen our connection to the Creator of the universe. We had a deep spiritual and joyful life that we shared together. I did not feel the need of a man to fulfill me spiritually. I was, however, happy and honored that I could bear children with Jacob and such beautiful children as well. My son Asher was known to be the most beautiful tribe in all of Israel. And Gad—what good fortune he was.

Thank you for such wonderful messages. I would like to open the floor for some discussion with all of you. What may be most of interest to our readers is the loving relationship between the four of you. There does not seem to be the level of jealousy that one may expect for four women to be married to the same man. Was there not competitiveness between you?
Leah: There was no significant competitiveness or jealousy between us. We were mostly united. The love between all of us was solid and unshakeable. We each had grown up in the household of Laban, so we knew from the very beginning of our lives that we needed and depended on each other for survival. The great love between us sustained us throughout our lives and even until today.

In my early years, I may have wanted my husband to love me more, and more importantly, more fully acknowledge that I was indeed his soul mate, but it was not because I was competitive with my beloved sister. How could I not wish the best for her at all times! She had protected me from marrying Esau. I owe her my life. I ached that she was not blessed with children as I had been. I prayed for her every day of my life.

Rachel: We each had our challenges but these challenges enabled us to grow and become more worthy of being the mothers of this holy nation. What helped to unify us was that we were always clear that our purpose and fulfillment lay in our capacity to birth the Jewish nation. It was true that Leah wanted more time with my husband and I wanted more children. In the end, we each received what we wanted. And we were each grateful for the role that we each played in birthing this nation. That was more than enough.

Bilha: I was born out of the concubine relationship that Laban had with my mother, so I had no aspirations of being a full wife myself. That I was a peligish to this holy man and my sons were considered full tribes in this emerging holy nation was more than I could have dreamed for or wanted. I am eternally grateful for the friendship and love of my sisters, particularly the beautiful loving Rachel.

Zilpa: I was also born out of a concubine relationship that Laban had with my mother, so I had no aspirations of being a full wife myself. I really didn't want to be a peligish, but my beloved sister Leah requested me to bear children with her husband so I did. I'm happy that I was gifted with motherhood, but it never defined who I was. My relationship with Jacob/Israel was very limited. I had not the desire nor the need for more.

As a point of clarification, would one of you explain to our readers what the difference is between a peligish and a wife according to Jewish law?
Bilha: I would like to answer that because I was a peligish and the daughter of a peligish, as was Zilpa. Generally speaking, a wife has more status and privileges than a peligish. Rachel and Leah were full wives, and Zilpa and I were peligishim. A man must provide for his wife with shelter, clothes, and conjugal relations. He is not obligated to do so with a peligish. A peligish does not have the same rights, privileges, and protection. There is no binding contract between a man and a peligish as a man has with his wife. A man can leave the peligish without offering her financial protection. Zilpa and I did not, however, worry about our welfare, because we knew that our protection was due to our relationships with Rachel and Leah, more than it was with Jacob. And of course when we had sons, we knew that we would be honored and cared for as well.

Thank you. I would like to speak briefly about a traumatic event that happened in your life that was so important in defining the Jewish people: the selling of Joseph into slavery. For so many years, everyone believed that

Joseph was dead, killed by a wild animal. Later on, it was revealed that he had been sold into slavery by his brothers, the sons of Leah.

I understand that you, Rachel, were not in a physical body at the time, but still you must have some thoughts and feelings about what happened.

Rachel: Unfortunately, my husband Jacob inspired jealousy among his sons by publicly demonstrating greater love to Joseph than to his other sons. He even gave Joseph a special coat and treated him as if he would be his sole heir. It was his way to stay connected to me. My most beautiful, precious, glorious son Joseph was surely a prophet, for he received visions and dreams of the future that were eventually realized. When he shared his prophetic dreams with his brothers prematurely, their hatred and jealousy of him increased.

These visions confirmed to them that Joseph believed he would be their leader and that they would have to be subservient to him. That was more than they could bear. I am glad that I was not physically alive to witness the event.

Viewing this event from my heavenly domain, I knew, however, that all that took place was part of the Divine plan. Because my son was so holy and pure, he was sent on a mission that would take him to Egypt to free the souls who had been imprisoned by the impurity there. He was all the things his dreams informed him he would be.

I supported him as much as I could from my heavenly station. Though he faced great challenges in his life, my son Joseph was blessed and continues to be a source of blessing to all. He became the ruler of Egypt. He saved not only his brothers in the time of famine, but all of Egypt. I am so proud of him. I am eternally honored and grateful to have been his mother.

Leah: I was so saddened to hear of Joseph's death. It was so hard to lose my beloved sister and then her most precious child. Jacob was inconsolable. I saw him even less than before. I was personally anguished and devastated for the role that I might have played in fostering jealousy among my sons for Joseph. Their actions were wrong, yet I have faith and I know that Hashem (God) works in mysterious ways.

Joseph being sent to Egypt was surely part of the Divine plan because when he became the ruler of Egypt he was in a position to save our lives. Nevertheless, I am glad that my sons in time had the opportunity to do *teshuva* (repentance) for the terrible action of selling their brother into slavery. In the course of their lives, my sons each made mistakes but they also repented. I pray that they serve as models for all time that a person can do wrong but they can change and become better people than they were before.

Bilha: My sons, as well as Zilpa's, were not involved as this was really a battle between the sons of Leah and the sons of Rachel for supremacy.

Zilpa: There have been times throughout Jewish history when all the tribes were united. When there is unity, the nation of Israel is strong and Divinely protected. When there is divisiveness among the tribes, the nation is weak and vulnerable to external enemies. It really is that simple and clear.

CONCLUDING RESPONSE TO OUR MOTHERS RACHEL, LEAH, BILHA, AND ZILPA

(It is suggested that this be read out loud by the reader or group.)

> *We remain in great debt for the love and sacrifice you each made to be a mother of the Jewish nation. We stand today to acknowledge each of you as our spiritual mothers. Together you embodied different facets of the Shechinah, the Divine Feminine. We are inspired by each of you. Though your contribution has not been adequately acknowledged in the tradition, we know that it was your love as the mothers of the tribes that imbued them with beauty and strength to carry out the mission prescribed for them.*
>
> *Most importantly, you together model an example of the kind of sisterhood that women can have. There is so much more that we can do when we are united with other women than we could ever do alone. As women, we are a powerful force for good in the world. As women, we bring more love into the world.*
>
> *Help us to gather with and bond with other women so we can bring forth a new consciousness into the world that is more loving, gentle, and kind. May we do this in ways that are uniquely feminine, like you, our mothers did. May we draw down blessings upon ourselves, our loved ones and the entire world. May we keep our hearts open. May our tears of love and tears of sorrow arouse mercy and blessing in the world. Amen.*

PRAYER TO THE GOD OF MOTHER RACHEL, LEAH, BILHA, AND ZILPA

> *May I be blessed to follow in the footsteps of my holy mothers Rachel, Leah, Bilha, and Zilpa, to participate in the birth of a new consciousness that expresses greater connectivity and oneness in the world. May I be willing to*

undergo challenges in order to reveal the Shechinah in our midst. May the tears that I shed in my life be dedicated to this purpose.

What Quality of the Feminine Do We Learn from These Four Mothers?

We must first learn from these four women the power and importance of sisterhood. Because they were bonded together in love, sacrifice, and dedication to the mission of birthing the Jewish people, they were able to fulfill their holy purpose together.

There is a call in our time to strengthen the bonds between women. For many women, men may come and go in their lives, but friendships with other women endure throughout a lifetime and are often a source of unconditional love and support. Female relationships provide a mirror for the personal and spiritual growth for a woman that is quite different than what she experiences with a man. Through relationships with other women, each woman is encouraged to more fully develop her particular archetype but also to express the other archetypes as well, and experience a greater sense of wholeness within herself.

The four mothers each demonstrate important qualities of the feminine that every woman should embrace. From the selfless love and goodness of Rachel, the willingness to serve and learn of Bilha, the vision and focus of Leah, and the mystical joy of Zilpa, women are invited to find dimensions within themselves to express the range of attributes embodied by these women.

Which Archetype Are You?
The Rachel Archetype: The Moon-Identified Woman

Whether as wife, mother, or lover, women embodying the Rachel archetype in large part are defined and fulfilled by these relationships. Being a mother was so important to Rachel that she even cried to Jacob, "Give me children or I will die" (Gen. 30:1). When Rachel gives birth to Joseph and becomes lover and mother, she becomes the embodiment of the ultimate feminine energy and blessing.

Rachel is a model of holy selflessness and graciousness for all women. Archetypical-Rachel women are generally married, traditional, and feminine. They make everything and everyone around them feel beautiful. A woman who embodies the Rachel archetype and is married to a good man who can bring down the light of God is unusually radiant and beautiful no matter her age.

A woman is often compared to the moon. Generally speaking, many women have a special relationship with the moon because the time of her menses is often coordinated with the phases of the moon. A moon-identified woman like the Rachel archetype is beautiful and changeable, similar to the moon. Like the moon, she has no light of her own. She reflects the light of her husband, just as the moon reflects the light of the sun.

Not having light of her own is not indicative of low self-esteem, spiritual deficiency, or a lack of intrinsic worthiness for Rachel archetypes. It is actually the opposite, for it is necessary for a person on the path of holiness to be able to surrender one's sense of self so as to reflect the light of God. Being able to surrender is quite different than being a doormat. A person needs a rather elevated ego to be able to know when to surrender and receive. A Rachel-archetypical woman is beautiful and generous, and radiates a spiritual light through her that elevates all who are blessed to be in her orbit.

Leah Archetype: The Intellectual Assertive Woman

The Leah archetype depicts a woman whose soul ascends beyond attachments and relationships in this world since she can connect directly with God, the source of all love and light. Leah is the archetype of the independent woman, whether she is in relationship or not.

A Leah woman either works hard to cultivate her own direct connection with the Light or is naturally blessed with a more direct connection than most people have. On an ego level, she may still indeed want the love of a man to define her, but on a soul level, she finds this restrictive. Archetypical Leah women are the intellectual equals of men, and generally assertive sexually as well.

For example, we are told the story of how Leah purchased the sexual services of Jacob with a dudaim (fertility herbs). Leah often showed herself dominant in comparison to Jacob. The archetypical Leah is that of an independent woman who will do what she feels necessary to actualize her higher vision. Archetypical-Leah woman are strong, powerful, and loving. Visionaries who see the larger picture, Leah women are willing to orchestrate changes to help move themselves and others forward in accordance with their vision.

Bilha Archetype: The Humble Woman of Service

Bilha is the intellectual, spiritual, and sexual consort to Jacob. Her relationship with Jacob is about spiritual growth and otherwise receiving from the aspect of submission and dependence like Rachel. Archetypical-Bilha women are loving, generous, and frequently are drawn to learn Bible and mystical teachings with men whom they admire and view as more knowledgeable than they. Bilhas attend Bible classes regularly, read books, and listen to classes online.

In addition to learning, Bilha-archetypical women love to serve. Bilhas thus are also the women who are active in organizations, spearheading and/ or working devotedly for important causes because dedication to that which is higher and greater than oneself is meaningful to them. Bilhas enjoy being part of a community of like-minded people who share a common goal.

Zilpa Archetype: The Spiritual Mystical Woman

Women who embody the Zilpa archetype are those heavenly, beautiful, feminine, spiritual, free-spirited angelic souls who manifest all that is beautiful and holy seemingly effortlessly. Zilpas lift everyone up who is blessed to be around them. Zilpa archetypes offer the world a glimpse of the beauty and heart of the Divine Presence.

If you see a woman dedicated to a form of spiritual or mind/body practice that embodies the feminine like yoga, dance, massage, or meditation, she is accessing Zilpa. Archetypical-Zilpa women meditate, learn esoteric wisdom, and are joyful in themselves, happy to be in relationship with a man and equally happy not to be. Zilpa's consciousness is above that of Jacob and she has no need of him. She is sometimes referred to as the archetypical Goddess type. Her spiritual radiance is not from this world. But in her role as peligish, Zilpa is symbolic of the deep descent of the Divine into the natural world.

KNOW YOUR PARTICULAR ARCHETYPE AND EMBODY THEM ALL

A woman will be primarily either a Rachel (practical, modest, and grounded), a Leah (contemplative, mystical, and assertive), a Bilha (intellectual, submissive, and selfless), or a Zilpa (evolved, free-spirited, and detached) archetype. Even though most women embody aspects of several of the archetypes, knowing and accepting one's primary archetype as a woman is very helpful, healing, and even liberating. When a woman truly honors her primary archetype, she will be better able to appreciate the coherency of her life experiences. Simply stated, life makes more sense when you know your principal archetype and accept yourself as you are. All the material presented is to help the reader identify her archetype, or for the male reader the archetype of the women in his life.

Women are, however, multidimensional beings, so when a woman embraces, integrates, and expresses additional archetypes, she experiences wholeness and completion within herself. She completes the tikkun (fixing) of the feminine for herself and the world.

I have come to appreciate doing this throughout my own life. I go so far as to have four names that I use correlating to the four spiritual worlds and the four archetypes. When a friend calls me by all my names, I feel seen for who I really am.

For most of my life, but particularly when I was in my twenties and thirties when I felt the pain of being single the most, I identified with Leah. She was the unloved one, or the one who was not as loved. Not being in a committed relationship with a loving man and having had a few heartbreaking broken engagements, I was, like Leah, compelled to forge my own direct connection with the Divine.

I became an author, a Jewish spiritual teacher, and guide to many so I could share the Divine Light and connection I had accessed. I celebrated my independence and did not want to be economically or spiritually dependent on a man. But secretly, I confess that for much of my life I wanted to be a Rachel: the beloved, beautiful, and treasured one, much like Leah did in her lifetime.

When I have been blessed to be in a committed relationship with a man, I identify more with Rachel. I find myself spending more time on my physical appearance, even getting my hair and nails done religiously each week. It is important that I look beautiful in the eyes of my beloved as well as my own.

In my Rachel mode, I am willing to sit quietly beside or even behind the man and encourage him to shine. I seek my reflection in his love and deeply appreciate all the little gestures of caring he makes towards me. I still have to work hard, but my spiritual work is now more how to make myself smaller, and allow myself to open and to trust so as to receive the light and love from the man. Since we both understand that his work in the relationship is ultimately to bring pleasure to me, I want to build him up and elevate him so he can draw down more light to give to me, himself, and the world.

Though Rachel and Leah are the primary female archetypes, women also need to be open to Bilha and Zilpa. I have embodied the Bilha archetype for most of my adult life as well. I have been blessed to learn Kabbalah with men who are more knowledgeable than I. Some have been brilliant and teachers in their own right. Men seem to like learning Kabbalah with me because I offer a feminine perspective and am able to draw out deeper learning for them than they might access themselves.

When I am in my Bilha archetype, I serve my synagogue, the Jewish community as a whole, and my friends. In my early adult years, I used to spend ten to fifteen volunteer hours a week serving my synagogue and organizing Shabbat and synagogue activities for my primary teacher, Rabbi Shlomo Carlebach of blessed memory.

Lastly, I am happiest when I am embodying the archetype of Zilpa. I am very much in my Zilpa when I am meditating and praying, especially in holy places in Israel. When I am teaching meditation, guiding myself and others to soar to great spiritual heights, I am accessing my Zilpa. When I am in my Zilpa, wherever I am, my soul is very expanded. My experience is that I barely exist, there is only God, and I experience myself as an expression of God. My Zilpa consciousness is more connected to the inner worlds that are revealed in meditation where there is no limitation or restriction, only love, joy, holiness, and truth. I am not always living as an embodiment of Zilpa, but am grateful for the times when I do, as I imagine the people around me are as well.

What Spiritual Practice Do We Learn from Rachel and Leah?
The Spiritual Practice of Holy Tears

Rachel and Leah were the masters of holy tears. From them, we as women (or men) in touch with the feminine within ourselves, learn how to shed tears that are healing to ourselves and the world. With her eyes tender from crying, Leah changed her destiny and birthed six tribes to become a mother of the Jewish people. As a mother who cares for each of her children, Mother Rachel is said to cry holy tears that offer protection and blessing to the Jewish people until they are all returned to the Land of Israel and there is peace. Jews go to the grave of Mother Rachel before Rosh Hashanah as well as throughout the year to beseech her to cry for their personal welfare as well as the welfare of the Jewish people.

Weeping is actually an important spiritual practice. The Zohar states that, "there is no gate that tears cannot enter." Tears atone for sins, misdeeds, and tears purify and open gates of blessing. If one weeps in prayer, one arouses Divine mercy upon oneself and all of Israel. To weep in prayer is a sign of a vulnerable and open heart, not of weakness.

Unfortunately, many of us have grown up being told to not honor or feel the feelings that we do. Consequently, we learn at an early age how to defend ourselves against our feelings. As a result, we avoid living our lives on a level of soul depth and connection that would be otherwise possible for us. We therefore cry less frequently or deeply.

Due to inevitable challenges in life circumstances, most of us at some time in our lives will be forced to feel painful and sad feelings. All challenges must be seen as spiritual opportunities. However, if we seek to distract or diminish our suffering with alcohol, television, sex, drugs, or food, we will not be able to extract the spiritual gifts within our pain. At these times, we need to remember that it is natural and good to allow ourselves our feelings of sadness and grief when they are triggered. Allow them be a springboard for healing and growth.

There are two types of crying. There is the unholy crying that comes from obsessing on negative thoughts. This crying often leaves one drained, exhausted, and feeling sorry for oneself. It is actually an expression of anger turned inward that blocks the flow of healing and blessing to oneself. And then there is holy crying, a crying that comes from deep in the soul. Holy tears purify, heal, and strengthen us. They may be viewed as a portable mikvah (ritual bath) that cleanses the soul. It is helpful to distinguish between these styles of crying so as to facilitate a shift within oneself to redemptive and cleansing holy tears that release pain and open the heart.

Women have been generally endowed with the gift of holy tears: tears of sadness and tears of joy. A woman's heart typically is more sensitive than a man's so she is inclined to cry more easily and frequently. A woman should not be embarrassed for the tears that she authentically sheds. Rather than repress or suppress their weeping, a woman or a man in touch with the feminine should be encouraged to discover and explore the source of their crying at its spiritual root.

If we allow ourselves to honor our pain and venture deeply into the tears, we will discover that our tears are not essentially personal. Within every loss, trial, or betrayal are the tears for the lack of God's realization in the world. The true reason that we cry, our souls cry, is because God's Presence, the Shechinah is not fully revealed in this world. When our personal losses become a portal to weep for the Shechinah, our tears become holy. Within the tears of the woman are the tears of the Shechinah Herself.

As such, the tears of a woman must be honored and treasured rather than ridiculed or mocked. The tears of a woman have the awesome power to arouse a blessing of Divine love and compassion and water the seeds for a fuller expression of beauty and balance in the world. When a woman cries for the Shechinah and allows the Shechinah to cry within and through her, her tears are healing to her and the world. A woman's tears can penetrate the heart of God and bring down blessings to the world. When women cry, they change reality. So a woman must be particularly careful not to use the power of her holy tears for personal manipulation. When we allow ourselves to feel the deep feelings within our own soul, to feel its grief, its sadness, its brokenness, paradoxically our pain is often lifted from us and we are made more whole. God heals the brokenhearted.

KEY QUESTIONS FOR REFLECTION AND DISCUSSION ON THE FOUR MOTHERS

1. The Zohar tells us that Rachel showed herself to be the reincarnation of Eve and Leah could be viewed as the reincarnation and the fixing of Lilith. Reflect and discuss some of the ways how you understand these associations. How do Rachel and Leah heal the rift between Eve and Lilith in this incarnation?
2. Of the four mothers, is there one with whom you identify most, and why?

Can you find aspects within yourself that resonate with each of the four women? Explore and share that with others.
3. Look at your closest women friends, and consider what archetype they most embody. Do you tend to be friends with women who are similar to you? How would you have to expand yourself to befriend women who are principally of a different archetype?

If you are a man reading this book, consider to which of the archetypes of the feminine you are most attracted. With which archetypes have you been in relationships? What archetype is your mother?

CHAPTER FIVE

DINA THE HEROINE
THE SECRETS OF OVERCOMING TRIALS AND TRIBULATIONS

When good things happen in life, when bad things happen in life, one must use all of one's experiences to deepen one's love, connection and appreciation for God. In this way, a person reveals the Light of God in the midst of darkness and evil.

—*Dina*

DINA

Dina, the one daughter of Jacob and Leah, has no spoken words of her own in the Bible. She is acted upon; she is talked about; she seems passive and wounded. Almost invisible, the Bible does not even mention her when Jacob blessed his sons on his deathbed. The brief paragraphs in the Bible devoted to her life are filled with violence unparalleled anywhere else in the Bible.

Dina is described in the Bible as "the daughter of Leah" because she went out to meet the young girls in the neighboring town. Just as Leah "went out" to initiate sexual relations with Jacob, her daughter Dina similarly "went out" to explore new horizons. Dina had only brothers and was lonely for the friendship of girls her own age. Shechem, the prince of the neighboring town that was named after him, had already seen Dina and was so drawn to her that he hatched a plan to abduct her. He cleverly brought timbrel-playing young girls within the hearing range of Dina and she was attracted to go out to hear the music and meet the young girls. Then, Dina, the first Jewish daughter born of a Jewish mother, was kidnapped and raped!

After the rape, Shechem tried to console her and appease her anger. He declared his desire to marry her. Chamor, the father of Shechem, along with Shechem then traveled to Jacob and her brothers to request Dina's hand in marriage. Chamor offered a large amount of money and proposed that intermarriage take place between the two communities. Nevertheless, he refused to release Dina. Knowing that they were unable to defeat them militarily to secure Dina's physical release, the sons of Jacob, Dina's brothers, came up with the following scheme to avenge the honor of their sister as well as rescue her.

The brothers agreed that marriages could take place between the two communities if the men in Shechem would become circumcised. Shechem and his father convinced the men in the town to accept this proposal by assuring them that they would each become wealthy as Jacob and his sons were very rich. All the men in the town surprisingly agreed to undergo this painful procedure immediately. On the third day, when the men were the weakest, Shimeon and Levi entered the town and rather than just kill Shechem and the men guarding Dina, they killed every man in the city and then they rescued Dina. They also looted the city because their sister had been defiled.

The actions that the brothers took to rescue Dina were troublesome to their father Jacob and probably are to many readers. It may, however, have been possible that the brothers only intended to kill Shechem so as to rescue Dina. The Jewish oral tradition tells us that Dina heard that there was a plot among the brothers of Shechem to slay Jacob's family after the circumcision and somehow she sent word to her brothers to warn them.

There are a few different accounts of what happened to Dina after the rape. In one account, she was so overcome with shame about what happened to her that she was reluctant to return to her family until her brother Shimeon persuaded her to return to live in his home as his wife. In another opinion, favored by Moshe Ben Maimon, known as Maimonides, the great Jewish thinker, she lived in Shimeon's house, not as his wife, but as a kind of widow. There is even another account that states that she married Job.

Of these different midrashim (legends), I chose one that resonates the most with me for the interview. Whether she married or she remained in Shimeon's home for the rest of her life is not central to our understanding the importance of Dina's story. From that night of rape, Dina became pregnant and bore a daughter named Osnat.

The legend is that Osnat was adopted by Potiphar and was raised by the wife of Potiphar, the same woman who tried to seduce Joseph. When Joseph refused the sexual advances from the wife of Potiphar, she accused him of rape and he was sent to the dungeon for twelve years. Later when Joseph was freed and ruling Egypt, he married Osnat, her daughter and his niece. Ultimately, Dina's story is one of redemption. See Bible, Genesis 34:1–31)

INTERVIEW WITH DINA

Dina, it is such an awesome honor to be in your presence. Do you have an initial message for women and men today?
Dina: God is good and is gracious to all of creation. Know this as a basic truth. Events may happen in your life and that of the world that seemingly do not look or feel good, but have faith—look beyond, look deeper, and you will find that it is all good. God is good and everything that takes place is all part of the Divine plan. So it is all good.

You were raped at a young age. Your child was taken from you by your father. How did you come to understand all of this in a positive light? How can that be good?
Dina: Of course, at the time I was totally devastated and deeply ashamed of myself. Did I deserve this to happen to me? I wondered whether I was guilty of

some crime from another lifetime. I was so young and had not done much in my life yet. I simply wandered off because I was lonely and wanted to play with some girls my own age. I had only older brothers. My biggest mistake was that I did not ask my family if I could go. I had not even told my family what I wanted to do. I just went.

That was wrong on my part. I didn't realize how important I was to my family. My brothers did not abandon me. They rescued me, and assured me of my honor and value. My mother loved me. I was forgiven for wandering off the property of the Jewish people and chose to stay close to my family for the rest of my life. That was indeed a great blessing for me.

Yet, how did you keep your faith in God through this incident? Many people also have terrible things happen to them, seemingly through no fault of their own. Do you have a message for them too?
Dina: As I grew older and more mature, I came to understand that all that happens in life is really Divine providence. God is good and all that happens is good. This is a deep truth that everyone must internalize deeply into one's heart. When good things happen in life, when bad things happen in life, one must use all of one's life experience to deepen one's love, connection, and appreciation for God. In this way, a person reveals the light of God in the midst of darkness and evil. There is always good in everything, even though it may not be immediately clear. Remember that I am, after all, the daughter of Leah and Jacob, so it was important for me and everyone that I demonstrate this truth for all to witness.

I also took responsibility for making a bad choice. For that, I suffered immediately. I quickly learned what I needed to learn, but that is not why this incident happened. I came to know that I was being used by God for a holy purpose. This incident, even though it was unpleasant, became a blessing to me and to the Jewish people.

What was the holy purpose?
Dina: As you can clearly see, there is a war in the universe between the forces of good and evil. I was simply a soldier in one of the battles. After Shechem raped me, he thought he loved me and wanted to marry me. His father appealed to my father and brothers for my hand in marriage, as if the rape never happened.

Rape was so commonplace there, no apologies were offered, but for the Jewish people it is a horrible crime. My brothers, wanting to avenge my honor and rescue me, came up with a scheme that marriages between our peoples could take place when the men of Shechem were circumcised. Surprisingly, they quickly agreed to this painful procedure and converted to Judaism. Because of what happened to me, the souls of the people of Shechem reincarnated as Jews in their next life. So it was really a blessing for them. Their power to cause future harm to God's world was mitigated, so that was very good too.

But you were harmed, weren't you?
Dina: Shechem may have raped my body, but not my soul. Yes, I was initially harmed, I was emotionally devastated, but I was also spiritually transformed. Because of what happened to me, I understood at an early age that I am not limited to my physical body. I have a beautiful soul. That is what is most important in life. My soul was actually elevated by this event. This is true for all who have had a crime or an offense committed against them. Whatever negativity you may have gathered in your life, you have been actually greatly cleansed through the difficult experience you have endured. You did not consciously choose for terrible things to happen, but God had compassion on you and determined that this was the best way to remove blockages to your own soul.

Is there anything more that you would like to say about yourself?
Dina: After the rape, I felt so ashamed and unworthy. I feared that I would be judged harshly by my family for leaving the family compound. My brother Shimeon persuaded me to live in his home after the rape. So grateful for his kindness, I lived out the rest of life within the confines of his tribe.

Did you ever marry?
Dina: Because of what happened to me, I had no desire to marry and bear additional children of my own. I made that decision early in my life. Besides, I was busy with the extended family. Being an aunt to so many children was a great joy and yet it did not take up the same amount of time as having a child of my own. Not bearing children, I could devote more time in developing myself spiritually, so as to have the Divine Presence rest upon me. My mothers, Leah and Zilpa, my mother's handmaiden, instructed me on how to be strong, how to be holy, and how to embody the Divine Presence in the most beautiful way.

Because of the love of my entire family, I felt blessed to simply be a Jewess. God was such a source of love and comfort for me. I do not want people to feel sorry for me. I am not a victim. There are no victims in God's world.

You, however, became pregnant from that one night of sexual relations with Shechem. Your daughter was taken away from you. Was that not difficult for you to bear?

Dina: Yes, that was very hard. Losing Osnat was a great loss. She was so beautiful and innocent. Because I was so young, my father determined that adoption would be the best option for a child born from a rape. He placed on her a special necklace with an inscription of the name of God upon it that later helped to identify her. At the time, I had no choice but to defer to his wishes and pray with all my heart that my child would be safe and protected. God must surely have a great plan for her. She was, after all, a Jewess, my daughter.

I was greatly blessed to meet her later in my life when the family immigrated to Egypt because of the famine. Can you imagine my delight after so many years to find that Joseph, my beloved brother, was ruling Egypt and had married my beautiful daughter?

God is so good. What a beauty my daughter was. We loved each other instantly and completely. Through her, I was fulfilled and doubly blessed as she was blessed to bear two beautiful sons, Manasseh and Ephraim, who became full-fledged tribes of Israel. It was then totally confirmed for me that everything that happened to me, to Joseph, to Osnat, was part of the Divine plan. We were blessed to be a part of it all.

You and your brother Joseph seem to have had a special bond. You were attacked in Shechem, and he is buried there. Could you offer some words to explain this?

Dina: As you remember, my mother Leah was pregnant with another son and prayed that the fetus become a girl so she would not embarrass her sister Rachel, my aunt. My mother then gave birth to me and Rachel gave birth to Joseph. Joseph and I were twin souls. We had a common destiny.

Even though I did not see him much growing up, I have a special love and connection to him. My beautiful holy brother Joseph was able to transform Egypt and soften the Divine judgments against them. He also graciously provided food for the entire Jewish people when it became necessary for us to travel to Egypt. Because of Joseph's stature, the Jewish people were given the finest land. When the Jewish people finally left Egypt, millions of Egyptians went with them and converted to Judaism. This is in part due to the merit of Joseph and all the good will he inspired among the Egyptian people. It is part of the Divine plan that there always are windows of opportunity given to the people of the nations of the world to become Jews.

Just as it was the Divine plan that I be raped in Shechem, it was also the Divine plan that my beautiful holy brother be buried in Shechem. Joseph's body could have been brought to Jerusalem or another place, but he requested burial in Shechem. The city of Shechem is a vortex of evil in the world. Joseph's tomb has been violated by Muslims numerous times because they cannot tolerate the Divine light that radiates from his tomb. Even murders of young Jews attempting to pray by his grave have occurred in your times.

Joseph, as a tzaddik (a righteous person), continues to work in the spiritual realms to mitigate the evil that takes place in the physical world. That is why he is physically buried in Shechem. Without his blessing, life in Israel would be even more difficult.

Do you have any final words for men and women today?

Dina: My heart is with all those who have suffered through no or little fault of their own, as I did. Forgive yourself. Forgive others. Release any anger or guilt you are holding. It only hurts you.

It is impossible to understand why bad things happen. Know that your soul has undergone a great soul correction through your affliction that is redemptive to you and to all of creation. May you be blessed to appreciate the spiritual gifts that have been given to you. Thank you for hearing my story. Love and blessings to all.

PRAYER TO THE GOD OF MOTHER DINA

(It is suggested that this be read out loud by the reader or group)

> *May the God of Mother Dina inspire me to grow and heal through the challenges I face in life. May the God of Mother Dina inspire me with the courage to transmute whatever negativity I have experienced into good. May I choose light over darkness, unity over divisiveness, good over evil, so as to reveal the Shechinah (Divine Presence) and the intrinsic beauty of life.*

What Quality of the Feminine Does Dina Embody?

Dina embodies the wisdom and open-heartedness of the feminine that enables a person to find and experience light amidst the greatest darkness. Such a person is not contaminated or tainted by the evil perpetuated upon her. Just like the Shechinah, dwelling in the midst of a world that seeks to deny Her very existence, such a person as Dina exhibits a beauty and dignity that is untouched by events on the earthly plane. She lives more internally than externally.

Though Dina experienced an early trauma that scarred her life, I don't believe she would be bitter, nor would she ever lose faith in the goodness of life. Dina reminds us that we too can overcome life challenges that may make us feel initially bitter or resentful.

The name Dina actually means "judgment." Her mother Leah judged that she was given too much blessing in having a seventh son, so she prayed that the fetus be changed into a female. Dina carried a spiritual burden of being a male who had been changed into a female.

Though she may not have consciously chosen her destiny, Dina courageously embodied the aspect of Divine judgment for herself and her people. Dina models to us how to rise above the limiting aspects of judgment to find Divine mercy and compassion for ourselves as she did.

A SPIRITUAL PRACTICE ATTRIBUTED TO DINA

The rape of Dina is yet another expression of the violation of the Divine Feminine. So remember Dina, light a candle for her and for all women who have been violated and oppressed. Pray sincerely for the redemption of the Shechinah from Her exile.

KEY QUESTIONS FOR REFLECTION AND FOLLOW-UP DISCUSSION ON DINA

1. Does the story of Dina resonate with you? Write or share with another person about a "negative" experience that you have had and how it changed you. Have you come to terms with it? Or are you still holding on to feelings of hurt, anger, grief? If you are meeting with others, take turns sharing with each other. One person is the speaker; the other person just listens fully, without judgment or giving advice. "The story of Dina resonates with me because _____."

2. If you were a victim of a crime or had and/or are currently experiencing a health challenge or another personal trial, and you still have questions about why it happened and what you could learn from this challenge, imagine that God can speak to you to comfort you right now. Take a few breaths to center yourself, and then take a sheet of paper and begin a sentence with the following words: "This is what I want to say to you…" and keep on writing from your higher consciousness without editing too much with your mind. This is only for you, and you do not have to share it unless you want to do so.

3. Were the brothers right to murder all the men in the town of Shechem? Is it correct to do a preemptive strike against those who seek to kill you? Were the inhabitants guilty by association because they did not protest but rather participated in the mistreatment and rape of women? Is this story relevant to our times?
4. Rape is a crime about power rather than passion, and yet women are often accused of instigating this crime. If a woman dresses immodestly, she may even be accused of asking to be raped. In a Muslim country, women may be jailed, punished, even executed when they are raped. Why? Take time to discuss the power dimensions of this crime and how rape can be prevented.
5. Why do you think that Dina is called the daughter of Jacob only after the rape? She was previously referred to as the daughter of Leah.

CHAPTER SIX

MIRIAM'S VISION
SEEING LIFE'S POTENTIAL AND PERFECTION

My dear sisters and brothers, do not feel limited by what appears in front of you. I never saw things as they appeared to be, but only as they would be in a more perfected state. Do not dwell on what is lacking in your life or in the world. Believe in your dreams, trust your passion and pay attention to what makes you excited and enthusiastic. Say yes to life and claim your spiritual ticket to the new world that is unfolding before you.

—*Miriam*

MIRIAM
PROPHETESS AND VISIONARY

More than any other woman in the Bible, Miriam, sister of Moses and Aaron, prophetess and visionary in her own right, emerges in modern times as a symbol of the rising of the feminine. Many books have been written about her within the last decade. A cup of water in her honor has been added to the Passover Seder by feminists in the 1990s. For thousands of years, her legacy as a prophetess and spiritual leader of the Jewish people was relatively unknown and unacknowledged. Miriam speaks very few words in the Bible and very few words are written about her. As with many women in the past and in the present who have labored behind the scenes, Miriam's contribution has been largely hidden.

When we learn about Miriam, it is important to keep in mind that Miriam demonstrated spiritual leadership as a woman. She did not imitate the masculine, as women often do when they move into positions of leadership. Throughout her life, Miriam embodied the intuition and the wisdom that is characteristic of the feminine.

Her style and her message were radically different than that of Moses because she was a woman. In addition to being a prophetess and the spiritual leader for the women in Egypt and in the desert, she was also a mother, a wife, a sister-in-law, and aunt. Her relationships informed her work. As most women do, Miriam valued all her relationships. Miriam is the only woman in the Torah said to have died with a kiss, which meant that the angel of death had no dominion over her soul. Her soul simply lovingly left her body.

Though the actual circumstances of her birth were not recorded, Miriam was born during the time when the Egyptians began to enslave the Jewish people. Her name Miriam comes from the Hebrew root *maroor*, which means "bitter," referencing the bitter hardship of the time in which she was born.

By the time Miriam was only five years old, her role as a prophetess, visionary, and a guiding light for the Jewish people was already revealed. According to the Jewish oral tradition, with courage, faith, and at risk of her own life, five-year-old Miriam and her mother disguised themselves as midwifes to birth both male and female babies in defiance of Pharaoh's decree. When brought in for questioning before Pharaoh as to why the male infants survived under their midwifery, Miriam and her mother stood up bravely and continued their holy work without concern for their personal safety. This act of civil disobedience on the part of these two brave females may have been the first recorded moral challenge to a tyrannical government.

Miriam was always the loving older sister and protector of her brother Moses. When her brother Moses was born, it was clear to all that this was the child about whom Miriam had prophesied. The Bible simply tells us that this child was "good." Legends tell us that the entire house was filled with spiritual light upon his birth. When it was no longer possible to hide Moses, he was placed in a basket in the water and Miriam watched him from the shore. As soon as Pharaoh's daughter "drew" him from the water, Miriam was instantly there to help her.

"Shall I go and summon a wet nurse from the Hebrew women who will nurse the boy for you?" Miriam inquired, never revealing that she was the sister of the child found in the water. Because of Miriam's intervention, Moses was nursed by his own mother who even received money to do so.

As Miriam grew, she became the spiritual leader of the women in Egypt and throughout the desert journey. Whenever the Jewish people traveled in the desert, they would not move unless Miriam, Moses, and Aaron were in front of them. There are many instances throughout the Torah that point to the spirituality and contribution on the part of the women that may be directly attributed to Miriam's leadership.

It is interesting to note that Miriam herself was not married until late in life. Said to be sickly looking with a green color to her complexion, she was passed over by the men looking for a mate, even though, or perhaps because, she was the sister of Moses and the leader of the women. Eventually, Miriam married a righteous man named Calev, said to be forty years her junior.

Throughout her life, even when she was single, Miriam was a strong advocate for women and their right for marital relations. Her advocacy is most well-known from an incident with Zipporah, the wife of Moses. When Miriam becomes aware that Zipporah was hurt because Moses no longer engaged in sexual relations with her, Miriam advocates for her. In a conversation with her brother Aaron, she criticizes Moses for abstaining from sexual relations on religious grounds.

"Has God only spoken to Moses? Hasn't He spoken to us and we continue normal marriages" (Num. 12:2). For criticizing Moses, Miriam was afflicted with tzara'as, a kind of skin affliction resembling leprosy. From this episode with Miriam, the sages of Israel inserted in the daily and Sabbath prayer book a reminder of what happened to Miriam so as to encourage everyone to be mindful of their speech each day.

It is also important to note that when Miriam died, no mourning on the part of the Jewish people was recorded as was with her brother Aaron. With her death, however, the source of water that had accompanied and nourished the Jewish people as they wandered in the desert mysteriously dried up. It was only then that the people realized that it was due to the merit of Miriam that there was water in the desert. It might have been the Lubavitcher Rebbe who commented that because the Jewish people did not shed tears over the loss of Miriam, the water dried up. As with many women, Miriam's contribution was not adequately appreciated until she was no longer living.

Throughout her life, Miriam was always connected to water. She stood by the water to watch her brother. She danced through the Red Sea. And most importantly, the rock that magically produced water for the Jewish people through the desert was given in the merit of Miriam.

For more information about Miriam, read the following chapters: Exodus 15:20, Numbers 12:1–16.

INTERVIEW WITH MIRIAM

It is such an honor to hear your wisdom and guidance. Do you have an initial message to people today?

Miriam: Dear ones, you live in most auspicious times. I am happy to share with you my wisdom and make myself energetically available to you. People in your time live with challenges and opportunities that are similar to when I lived in a physical body. Whether you know it or not, many of the souls inhabiting human bodies today are actually reincarnations of people who lived in my time as well those who have volunteered to return to assist the world during this awesome time of transformation. Just as we were moved in the most radical way into a new reality at the time in which I physically lived, you are similarly on the edge of a new frontier of consciousness.

Get your tambourines ready! I want you to know that there will be much to sing and dance about in your time.

Please continue. What you are saying is so exciting!

Miriam: Consider for a moment what an amazing period of time it was when I occupied a physical body. Through wondrous signs and many miracles, the Jewish people were brought out of the enslavement of Egypt. Prior to leaving Egypt, we lived through ten awesome plagues. With every plague, physical reality crumbled before our eyes, yet it also brought forth a deeper revelation of Godliness that inspired faith on our part. Our hold on reality as we knew it withered away as we witnessed the ten plagues, saw locusts appear, the Nile River turn bloody, and many other supernatural occurrences. There literally was nothing physical to hold on to. We had to put our trust in a God that we could not see or touch. This was quite new for many Jews who were assimilated and spiritually were not so different from the Egyptians. Many Jews who did not prepare their homes by pouring blood on their doorposts from the slaughter of the lamb perished during the last plague. Those deaths were devastating to those who remained. We all lost loved ones. Then, we had to leave Egypt and all that we knew to journey into the desert. We quickly baked matzah.

In what way is our time similar to your time?

Miriam: Your time is also awesome. People in your time whose consciousness is limited to a materialistic view of reality will have a very challenging time, as did those in mine. For those of faith, it will be a glorious time as it was for us. Please understand that there will be both hardship and spiritual opportunity as your world undergoes a time of transmutation. Floods, plagues, earthquakes, drought, war, and terrorism occurring in many places in your world will help awaken people to the deeper reality of how interconnected all of life is.

Because of your technological advances, the world is informed quickly about what is happening everywhere. It will become increasingly difficult to dismiss the suffering of others that you see presented on television or read about in newspapers and on the Internet as not affecting you personally. People will more fully realize how interconnected and truly vulnerable they are.

I do not say this to alarm you but rather to help you prepare for the challenges before you. When the world is undergoing a major change and transformation, it will be natural to feel worried and frightened by all that is taking place. You may feel like life is out of control, but know that it is not. Divine order is being restored. Do not be afraid with the changes that occur around you. Find your peace within yourself and in your relationship with God.

What do you predict for our time?

Miriam: That which you have longed for in the deepest recesses of your heart and soul will soon be upon you. You will see, feel, and experience God in a way that was not possible for you before. Lift your consciousness beyond what is happening on the physical plane of existence. Let go of materialism as a definition of your life. Cast away doubt and fear. Pray to God for protection, guidance, and wisdom.

It is very easy in your time for everyone to turn to God, so be happy and grateful. Know that everything that is happening in your life and in the world is to prepare and purify you for a deeper revelation of God. You will also each learn firsthand as people did in my time that there is nothing in the world that can offer you protection but God. God is your deepest truth and reality. Rejoice, for all you need is simple faith. With faith, you draw to yourself an angelic force field that will protect you. Your time is actually a very glorious time to be alive.

Miriam, you were a prophetess. You were blessed with holy vision to know what was going to happen from the time you were a child. At the age of five, you persuaded your father, the leader of the Jewish people, to reverse a decree he had issued. Would you tell us more about this?

Miriam: My father had divorced my mother because of Pharaoh's decree that male infants be killed at the time of their birth. Because my father was the head of the Jewish people, all the Jewish men also divorced their wives so as to not have any children. I confronted my father. I told him that his decree was even worse than Pharaoh's because it was against the birth of all children, male and female. It was not right that my father, the leader of the Jewish people, should be afraid of Pharaoh. I also knew that my parents would birth the future redeemer of the Jewish people so it was necessary that they remarry and resume sexual relations.

With holy chutzpah, when I was five years old, I told my father, "Do your part, trust, and God will do His."

What happens to people as a result of the choices they make is in the hands of God. This is still my message to all. Do the right thing. Do what God wants you to do. Do not compromise yourself and make choices from a place of fear rather than faith and trust in God.

How do we simple people develop faith?

Miriam: Faith is a part of every person, available and integral to the well-being of a person. Faith is not blind as people often say, but it is a higher level of knowing that is actually hardwired into the core of your being. Give yourself time to meditate and pray each day. Your consciousness will soon be refined and lifted upward to greater awareness of God. When you experience God, you access the faith and the love that is your birthright.

Sing and dance each day. Do kind deeds to people around you. Take time each day to receive guidance, wisdom, and direction from within. Be happy. You have each been given a soul compass to guide you. The more you listen and trust your intuition, the greater your capacity to receive accurate information and holy wisdom from the higher spiritual realms.

My dear sisters and brothers, do not feel limited by what appears in front of you. I never saw things as they appeared to be, but only as they would be in a more perfected state. Do not dwell on what is lacking in your life or in the world. Believe in your dreams, trust your passion, and pay attention to what makes you excited and enthusiastic. Say yes to life and claim your spiritual ticket to the new world that is unfolding before your very eyes.

You have become a symbol to many women today seeking to claim their spiritual power as women. Would you speak about the role of women at this time?

Miriam: Since the beginning of time and until the end of time, women have always had and will always have a most important role and a special responsibility to guide humanity toward its highest good. For many women, this sacred role takes place primarily in the context of the family. As a mother, a woman is a child's greatest spiritual teacher, responsible for transmitting to her children, and even to her husband, the innermost secrets of the divinity of life.

What an awesome and holy assignment the Holy One entrusted to women. For many women, the sacred role of care taking and soul guarding extends into the community and outward toward the entire world.

Everyone must know that it has always been and will always be the wisdom, the love, the intuition, the faith, and even the heroism of women throughout time that has sustained the humanity of all civilizations. The particular influence of Jewish women on safeguarding the purity of the nation of Israel is immeasurable. Quite simply, there would be no Jewish community if not for the courageous actions of women. As a woman, you need to remember and claim this legacy as your own. The work of women in the past may have been more private than public, but just because these women were not validated publicly does not make their work less worthwhile or important. Besides, the greatest spiritual work can only be performed in privacy.

Today, many women are working outside of the home in addition to raising children.

Miriam: Your current world is quite unique for women for it is only in your time that the majority of women have entered into the general marketplace. Most women until recently were spared from having to enter the public arena, so they could better nurture and more fully develop feminine sensitivities in a more sheltered setting.

The challenge for a woman in your time is to maintain access to the gifts and talents that have been given to her because she is a woman, even when she is in the world of work outside of the home. Women in your time must be quite careful to not confuse power with influence. Power for its own sake diminishes the sanctity of women. Who you are as a woman, wherever you are, impacts on others, more than you can ever know.

As a woman, did you not feel marginalized by Moses? Many people suspect that there was a power struggle between the two of you.

Miriam: No, there was no power struggle between us. I always loved my brothers. Moses was chosen to be God's intermediary to the people. Most of the people were awed by Moses and did not find him approachable. Remember, Moses had not lived with the people as Aaron and I had. Even when he was living in their midst, most of the time Moses was in meditation. Aaron and I were the indigenous leaders of the people who were intimately involved in their lives. I was responsible for the women from all the tribes.

In many instances, recorded and not recorded, Moses recognized that he could not on his own address the needs and concerns of the women. When Moses did not know what to do with the women, he either asked me or God and received an answer.

I was plenty busy caring for and advocating for the women. The women have much to be proud of, for it was the women who provided the stability and the support for the spiritual and physical sustenance of the entire people during the desert experience.

What did the women do in the desert?

Miriam: There are so many examples of the holiness and righteousness of the women, too many to enumerate all of them with you now. But what may be the most outstanding testimony to the greatness of the women was that the women did not participate in the sin of the Golden Calf. They withheld their jewelry, though sometimes it was taken from them against their will. Their lack of participation in the Golden Calf was not because they were stingy. You see how they contributed generously to the building of the Mishkon, the tabernacle for the Divine Presence in the desert.

There was a moral fiber within women during the desert experience that was unique to them. The women in the desert also did not participate in the numerous rebellions against Moses' authority and often discouraged their husbands from participating as well. When the spies were sent to visit the land of Israel prior to our entry into it, the women did not believe the negative reports about the land. It is generally accepted that it was due to the merit of the women that the Jewish people left Egypt and entered into the land of Israel. Even the male commentaries written about this time testify to this fact.

They also predict that it will once again be the merit of the women that will take the world forward in the times to come. I believe this as well.

So it is important that women in your time understand this. Women are generally on a higher spiritual level than men so it is actually the women who must guide humanity forward. Women have always done this in the past and must also do so in the future.

Why do you think that the women are on a higher spiritual level than the men?

Miriam: Women for the most part are more inwardly focused, intuitive, and naturally exhibit more faith than men. Every woman must know this about herself and claim the spiritual gifts of simply being blessed a woman. A woman's intuition is a real phenomenon and must be respected. A woman in touch with her feminine intuition is not limited or swayed by physical externalities for which men may be prone. It is therefore appropriate that a woman be called upon to offer guidance and vision because she can see more clearly what is revealed in the heart but hidden to the human eye.

As a general rule, a woman is more receptive to Godliness than a man. It is not because she is less than a man that she has fewer *mitzvot*, commandments or religious obligations. Actually, she needs fewer external obligations because she is inherently more pious than a man. Because a woman is heart-centered, she always seeks opportunities to love and embrace life and those around her wherever she is. She wisely seeks to improve herself first rather than change her circumstances. Her deep yearning for love keeps her open and receptive to higher spiritual frequencies.

But, did you not feel left out as a woman when the Torah was given on Mount Sinai to Moses?

Miriam: Before the Holy One gave the Torah to the Jewish people, God spoke separately to the women first and then to the men. This is coded in the Torah. The women are referred to as "the House of Israel." We women received all that we needed to be connected to God. It is true that I would have liked to be with Moses when he ascended the mountain, but I was not summoned. Only Moses, not even Aaron, was invited to ascend the mountain.

The Torah that you read in your time was channeled and written by Moses, so it primarily records what occurred through him. After the revelation at Sinai, Moses was responsible for recording the experiences of the desert and he did so from his vantage point. The subsequent commentaries on what Moses wrote were written by men primarily for men.

This whole rabbinic tradition that emerged later in time is directed to men because there is greater need on the part of men for this kind of structure of laws and learning than for women. Men have written many books that they study continually because it is more of the masculine nature to stand outside of life, analyzing, attempting to understand and control life. It is the nature of the feminine to live in the fullness of life. You call it "history" and not her-story for a reason.

If you look only at the written accounts, it may look like my authority was limited, but that is not an accurate, or rather, a complete representation of what occurred. My teachings have not yet been written down and will never be. Words can never capture the depths of the heart of the feminine. The path of feminine spirituality was and is only transmitted orally from mother to daughter and found through communities of women celebrating, singing, and dancing together.

What is the feminine path of spirituality about? What spiritual practices do you recommend to be on this path?

Miriam: The feminine path is all about the embodiment of Godliness within oneself and the revelation of Godliness within all of creation. Feminine spirituality is a celebration of the immanence of God. Very simply, masculine spirituality is about how awesome and separate the Divine is. Feminine spirituality is about how intimate and close the Divine is.

One spiritual practice that I advocate for men and women is dancing. Pray to God and dance each day. When we were living in Sinai, we held drumming circles almost nightly and we danced all the time. It was such a glorious time being in the desert all together. Many people may trivialize dancing believing it to be inferior to serious study. I do not think so. Dance offers a woman and a man in touch with his feminine a deeper connection to the Holy One than analytic study. To dance ecstatically before God is to live life fully. The deepest secrets of God are transmitted to the dancer who knows how to dance and be danced by the Divine Herself. You will learn all that you need to know through dance. You will learn to surrender, live authentically from the heart, and most importantly embody the Shechinah.

It is one thing to talk about God and quite another to experience God within one's own body. Meditate and pray while you dance. Allow yourself to be moved from deep within. Create drumming and dance circles with each other and make dance your spiritual practice. Do not underestimate the power of dancing to bring joy, peace, and wisdom.

You led the women in circle dances as they crossed the Red Sea. Why "circle dances"?
Miriam: The circle is the symbol of the feminine. A woman's body is full of circles for a reason. Have you not noticed that when women gather together they often form circles? Throughout time, there are always knitting circles, sewing circles, all kinds of women circles. Even when women gather in small groups to talk with each other, they naturally sit in the form of a circle. Women naturally feel most comfortable in circles. I guided the women to do circle dances when we crossed the Red Sea because I wanted to transmit to them then, as well as for posterity, this most direct experience of the Shechinah that is only possible to receive when in a circle.

Please explain more. What is so important about the circle?
Miriam: The circle has important spiritual properties that reveal much about the wisdom of the feminine. First, the circle has no beginning or end. There is no past and no future in the circle. The circle also reminds us that God is always the center and every point in the circle is equidistant from the center. While masculine energy is hierarchal and linear, feminine energy is circular, inclusive, and egalitarian.

Consequently, a woman in touch with the feminine does not look to others for spiritual direction but only inwardly to the God within her. Her circular vision enables her to see in all directions the oneness all around her. Through circle dances, a woman learns, embodies, and teaches the world that every person is equally important. Everyone is beloved. Without each person in the circle, there would be a hole. Dancing or sitting in a circle also reminds a woman ultimately to be a vessel and create holy vessels in her life as well. So, when we women danced in circles, it was to embody these deep teachings.

The song you sang that is recorded in the Bible was a very succinct song in the present tense, while Moses' song was much longer and sung in the future tense.
Miriam: The song of Moses was prophetic, revealing what will take place in the time period known as "the End of Days." It is therefore sung in the future

tense because this is the song that is to be sung for the time to come. What we experienced crossing the Red Sea was only a taste of the redemption that will come in the future when all evil will be obliterated and God is totally revealed through nature. My song was also prophetic, but it was more of a chant, brief, and sung in the present tense.

Why was your song short and sung in the present tense?

Miriam: One does not need many words to reveal a deeper truth. Actually, the fewer the words, the deeper the truth. At the crossing of the Red Sea, the women through the short chant and circle dances were able to draw down, reveal, and even embody higher supernal lights than Moses who was even singing about a future time. Feminine spirituality is always present tense. In the deepest truth, there is truly only the now.

The Divine Presence is only revealed in the present moment. Feminine spirituality is a perpetual celebration of the immanence of God, the Divine Presence, never based in what will be in the future, or what was in the past, but always in the present. The present is surely a present, by that I mean a gift.

Thank you. That returns us full circle to what we were discussing earlier about feminine spirituality. Is there another practice besides dancing and chanting that you recommend for women?

Miriam: Yes, indeed. Because women are moved more by love than men, they must also create times for communing with their hearts and sharing with each other. Learning to speak from the heart and to listen from the heart is yet another important feminine spiritual practice that nourishes a woman's contact with her soul.

Women are naturally intuitive and have been blessed with great internal inner knowing. Through the spiritual practice of sharing and communing with others, a woman will draw out of the spiritual wellsprings within her own very self the deepest secrets of God and creation that men can only read and study about in books. She has been blessed inherently with this profound inner knowing simply because she is a woman.

Why then do women try to be like men?

Miriam: You live in a time when the feminine is not sufficiently appreciated and is even devalued. Your highly technological culture gives greater emphasis to the head than to the heart or the body. Though the heart may be located below the head, it is not lower in importance.

Remember that it is the soul within a person that offers the highest guidance to a person. The heart and soul of a person are intertwined and must be honored as such. I remind you that it is actually pointless to try to figure out life with one's mind, yet so many people think that is what they are supposed to do.

Yes, I am quite dismayed when I see women valuing the masculine way over the feminine way. It doesn't make any sense to me. Why should a woman want to be equal to a man or like a man when she is superior to him in so many ways? When we lived in the desert, women were strong, united, and we celebrated ourselves as women, living our lives fully with our hearts and souls. We didn't want to be like men.

More and more women today want to do the same work as men do. Is that good? Women want to be doctors, lawyers, scientists, and so forth. They don't want to stay home and be housewives. To be home feels isolating to many women.

Miriam: It is okay for women to be out of the home as long as a woman remains in touch with her intuitive feminine wisdom. She can be whatever she wants to be, even the president of a country. I am simply concerned, however, that when women imitate men and abandon their own inner knowing of the feminine, the imbalance between the masculine and feminine in the world increases.

For thousands of years the world has been dominated by men in positions of power over other men and women. Just because women may be in positions of power does not mean that they embody the feminine, and rectify the imbalance between the masculine and feminine in the world.

Please tell us more about what you mean by the imbalance between the masculine and feminine.

Miriam: The world suffers due to this imbalance. Masculine energy has made tremendous accomplishments in the external world, for that is the nature of masculine energy; it is always expanding. Unfortunately, these accomplishments have occurred at the cost of the feminine.

For example, modern societies in your time have made great technological advances, but you lack intimate loving communities where people can be authentic, vulnerable, and caring with each other. It is the wisdom and the heart of the feminine that nurtures real intimacy between people. What happens in the home is what really makes a difference in people's lives. In every home, a woman must become a priestess, a prophetess, a visionary, a representative of the Divine Presence for her husband and her children.

What good is technological advancement if more and more people are depressed, anxious, isolated, and unhappy because of the lack of meaningful relationships with other human beings? Societies pay dearly for the imbalance between the masculine and feminine. So if women become more like men, who will do the nurturing needed to make a person feel totally loved and validated?

But what about women who have been terribly oppressed by patriarchal societies?

Miriam: I am deeply pained by the anguish, the torment, and even cruelty that many women have experienced. Yes, it is true; women have been oppressed by men and still carry a legacy of pain and inferiority that is often passed between mother and daughter. This is a most unfortunate burden that women have had to endure. It breaks my heart to have witnessed how men have dominated and oppressed women over time throughout the world. It is not what God wants.

When men are disconnected from God, they dominate and oppress women. Any man who is truly rooted in God honors and respects the wisdom of women. How a person treats a woman or women in general is a measuring stick of the Godliness of a person. The laws of Torah were made to safeguard and protect women from the aggressiveness that is inherent in the nature of man. Her sanctity as a woman must be protected. When the sanctity of women is violated, the society is in danger of losing its Divine blessing for sustenance and even survival.

What wisdom can you offer women who have been oppressed by men?

Miriam: Women, please do not see yourself through the lens of weak and insecure men who are actually afraid or jealous of your womanly power. As a woman, you are so beautiful and so radiant. Never forget that. No one can take that away from you. You must know this as your deepest truth.

I strongly recommend that each woman join or form a group with other women who will reflect back to you the beauty and wisdom of who you are as a woman. Your strength lies in community with other women. This was true for women when I lived in a body and it remains so for women for all time. Celebrate your blessings and gifts as women. You are more emotional than men but that is because you are more God connected.

Too often your gifts as women are devalued by men, and then you do not feel good about yourself. Do not define who you are from the feedback that you receive from men. When you need feedback and guidance, ask your women or girlfriends who love you. The women in my time were deeply connected to each other.

Before we conclude our time together, I would like to ask you about the unpleasant incident of tzara'as you were afflicted with that was recorded in the Bible. I heard in some Jewish circles that this affliction was a punishment for rebellion on your part against Moses.

Miriam: Contrary to what people may think, there was no need or desire on my part to rebel against my brother Moses. I was afflicted with tzara'as because I spoke badly about Moses to my brother Aaron. I only did so because I was deeply pained by Moses' abandonment of his marital responsibilities toward his wife Zipporah. She cried to me about this and my heart went out to her. I know this pain all too well. For so long I was not married so I know what it is to be without a man's love.

Everything that I know about sexual relations between a husband and a wife is that sex is holy. It is what God wants. We were created through sex and we create new life through sex. Still, our lovemaking is much more than procreation. It is a form of worship because we experience God so directly through sexual relations. As you can see, I am very passionate about this, as I believe every woman should be.

So you must understand how terribly upset I was that my brother Moses refrained from sexual relations with his wife when she desired this intimacy with him. Why should any women be deprived of this experience, especially Zipporah, who was a convert, alone, and separate from her biological family?

These were my thoughts and feelings. I was simply conferring with my brother Aaron to see if he shared my perspective about this issue. I am after all Moses' older sister and Aaron is his brother. I did not feel that there was anything wrong with my speaking to our brother about this matter. I found out differently. For the sin of *loshon hara,* speaking evil, I was quarantined for seven days outside of the camp. I experienced firsthand how important it is to be mindful of one's speech. Everyone in the community of Israel also witnessed and learned from what happened to me.

Why were you punished in this way?

Miriam: All punishments are metered out in proportion to the sin. Skin afflictions in the desert occurred with people who judged others superficially. Because they saw only the surface of a person, their skin, their surface, was afflicted. When I gossiped about my brother Moses and his private relationship with his wife, as if he was simply an ordinary man, I was punished.

My brother was more of an angel than a man, so I had no right to judge him by my standards of what is appropriate for a man. Thankfully, Moses quickly prayed for me, so I was spared and did not die.

What happened to you during this time of being quarantined from the rest of the people? It is said that you came back more radiant than you had ever been.

Miriam: I learned so much during this time of healing as anyone does when they experience an affliction or illness. In my case, it was clear to me, and to everyone, that mine came directly from God. This affliction brought me closer to God than I was before.

It was truly a gift. It peeled away layers that had kept me separate from God. As an older sister and as a leader of the women, I had always taken care of others before myself. Now during the precious time when I was quarantined, it was only me and God. Freed of my responsibilities to others, I went deeper in my experience of God. The Divine Presence took residence within my body in a way that did not happen before.

I never expected that my words about Moses would cause this affliction, but I learned so much about who my brother Moses was, who God is, and who I was, so I was deeply grateful.

At my request, my husband divorced me immediately as I left the camp so as to free me to be with myself without distractions and attachments. When I returned to the people, he remarried me. I was so happy, even happier than I had been when he married me the first time.

I had felt at the time of our first marriage that Calev, such a righteous man of compassion, married me because I was alone. Now with the Divine Presence shining and guiding me so fully, a greater and holier love and passion was awakened from my beloved Calev. This made me even happier than I'd ever been before.

From our joy, we birthed children, even in my old age. I had wanted children for so long, and after this tribulation and deeper prayer on my part, miracles occurred for me.

Do you have any guidance to others who are healing from an illness and affliction?

Miriam: God is your healer. This illness or affliction has come to help you in the way that your soul wants. Peel away the fear, the anger, the judgments that have separated you from others, from God, and from who you really are. Use this time of illness and affliction you have been given to grow spiritually. It is not random that you are challenged in this way. Examine your deeds carefully.

I was fortunate that I knew what caused my illness. It is not always so clear for many. Always, remember that God is your healer. The Divine Presence is with you always, but particularly when you are ill. It is very helpful that when you are sick that you give charity to others.

I offer all those who are suffering physically, emotionally, and spiritually my deepest blessings and love. May you heal quickly. Always remember that this physical world is not the only world. The next world, the World to Come, is filled with great joy for those who have drawn close to God when they were physically embodied.

Please make every moment count in your life while you live in a physical world. Your physical life is short and you never know when it will end. Remember that you cannot take your material possessions with you. You can, however, take with you your good deeds and your love of God. So, always make an effort wherever you are to give charity and do good deeds.

Any final words to people before you depart?
Miriam: During this brief time on the earthly plane, do good deeds to others. Be kind. Be grateful. Open and give your heart away each day. Love God. Love yourself. Love others. And dance, always remember to dance and celebrate the gifts of life that you have been given. Connect with me and the women of the desert when you sing and dance with your full hearts. The same ecstatic joy that we experienced is there for you too. I love you.

CONCLUDING RESPONSE TO SISTER MIRIAM
(It is suggested that this be read out loud by the reader or group.)

> *Thank you for your words of love and inspiration. You are and will always be a powerful model for so many of us. We are currently seeking new ways to express our love and help make this world a better place. Your words remind us of the unique role that women play in the world. We clearly know that we do not benefit ourselves or others by imitating men or envying their power. Admittedly, we have been shortsighted in honoring the masculine displays of power over the subtler feminine forms of influence.*

> *We are grateful for the unique gifts and talents given to us by virtue of being women. As women, we are connected to the wholeness of life. When we share the love within our hearts, we open the hearts of those around us so healing can occur. Our words are powerful and transformative. Like the women who lived in the desert under your leadership, may we also embody the feminine spirit and help heal this world as women.*

As you encouraged us so many times, we will seek to strengthen our community with other women. We will not be competitive with other women nor will we betray them. Our strength and healing comes through honoring ourselves and others. May we trust our feminine intuition. May we dance all the time. May we always have faith in the goodness of life. Amen.

PRAYER TO THE GOD OF SISTER MIRIAM

May the God of Sister Miriam inspire me to trust what I know deep inside me as my truth. I can trust my intuition. May the God of Sister Miriam give me the courage to go forward in my life expressing my vision and truth.

What Qualities of the Feminine Does Miriam Demonstrate?
1. **Honor your feminine intuition as Miriam did.**

Miriam is ultimately a visionary who inspires women and men with the faith to trust their intuition and not be limited to what they see happening in the physical world. There are still so many examples of Miriam's intuition that altered the destiny of the Jewish people that were not mentioned in the introduction and interview sections of this chapter.

For example, during the awesome time of departure of the Jewish people, Miriam "saw" the future and "knew" that a miracle was going to take place, so she persuaded the women to bring their tambourines when leaving Egypt. In place of taking other items that may have been practical and helpful for the journey, the women packed their tambourines as Miriam told them to do.

2. **Be in the present.**

Do not put off living until a future time. God is only experienced in the present, not in the future or in the past. Miriam demonstrated how the Divine Presence is only revealed in the present moment. Being present is a gift of feminine wisdom.

3. **Dance.**

Miriam taught the mysteries of the circle and feminine spirituality. When the Jewish people crossed the Red Sea, Miriam, the prophetess, the sister of Aaron, took the timbrel in her hand, and all the women went out after her with tambourines and with circle dances and Miriam answered them, "Sing to the Lord for he has triumphed gloriously; the horse and his rider has he thrown into the sea" (Ex. 15:21). Through her song and her simple circle dances, Miriam, ancient prophetess, heralded in a new paradigm of consciousness that embodied the power and vision of the feminine that is more revolutionary than the prophecy of Moses.

4. **Women's right to sexual intimacy.**
A woman's right to sexual intimacy was important to Miriam as most clearly demonstrated when Miriam advocated for Zipporah. Miriam is also credited with inspiring and encouraging the women in Egypt to engage in sexual relations, even at times when it was difficult and dangerous for them to bear more children. Under Miriam's leadership and guidance, the Jewish women in Egypt would not only feed their exhausted husbands a hot meal after a day's work, they would beautify themselves so as to seduce the men to have sexual relations with them. We are told that the women would polish their copper mirrors and use them to beautify themselves for their husbands. These holy mirrors traveled with the Jewish people and were lovingly donated by the women for the construction of the Mishkon, the holy tabernacle for the indwelling Presence of God.

By the way, Moses was initially reluctant to use the mirrors for they were an instrument for vanity, but he was told by God that these mirrors were holy and should be included in the Mishkon. Even though the resources to feed additional people were limited, under Miriam's counsel, the women trusted that God would provide for all and another mouth would not burden God. It was the women who had the strength, courage, and faith to birth children, even at risk of their own lives.

What Spiritual Practice Do We Learn from Miriam?
The Spiritual Practice of Dance

In the interview section, Miriam encourages women to dance. Many may think of dance as trivial, but Miriam explains that dance is a powerful spiritual practice for experiencing a revelation of Godliness within oneself. Every woman in touch with her feminine knows that singing and dancing give her faith, strength, and joy. It is one of the secrets of the feminine. Women need to remember to give themselves time to sing and dance with each other for it is there that they will find inspiration. If we can sing, dance, and play a tambourine and drum, in good times and challenging times, we can go forward in our lives.

Miriam also advocates that women allocate time for intimate sharing with each other. By this, women refine their capacities to listen, and be compassionate and loving. They receive the validation of these qualities of the feminine that they might not experience elsewhere.

Women support groups help strengthen a woman's capacity to offer her feminine gifts to herself, her relationships, and the world at large. Talking to one's female friends from the heart and soul, as is the nature of the feminine, is in itself a spiritual practice. It is not a waste of time by any means.

KEY QUESTIONS FOR REFLECTION AND FOLLOW-UP DISCUSSION ON MIRIAM

1. What traits did Miriam possess and demonstrate in her life that inspire you today? How can you increase your awareness of Miriam, the qualities she embodied, and the spiritual practices she recommended?
2. Do you see Miriam as a feminist or simply as a strong woman? Is there a difference?
3. Should women have their own separate prayer and learning spaces, or is it preferable that in modern times men and women are fully integrated in prayer services and learning?
4. Do you imagine that Miriam was upset when Moses chose Yeshoushah to be his successor, rather than her husband Calev, who was younger and one of the spies who returned with a good report of the land? Would it not have been more appropriate to select Calev rather than Yeshoushah?

CHAPTER SEVEN

BATYA'S REBELLION
THE COURAGE TO TRANSLATE VISION INTO REALITY

I always prayed to live a life of truth, purity, and integrity even if it was in conflict with everything I had known before. Living a meaningful and purposeful life was always my greatest goal. I knew that such a life offered to me the greatest riches, more than all the gold that I had in the palace.

—Batya

BATYA

Batya, the firstborn and adopted daughter of Amenhotep III, Pharaoh of Egypt, was acknowledged in the Bible as the mother of Moses, the redeemer of the Jewish people. Though Moses was not her biological son, Batya named him and raised him as her own. Batya was one of nine people who entered Paradise with full consciousness (Derech Eretz Zuta 1). Her soul had reached total perfection and her consciousness left her body at the moment of her choosing. She was freed from the necessity of reincarnation.

As the princess of Egypt, Batya was a mystic, adept with full entry into the esoteric knowledge, sorcery, and spiritual practices of Egypt. Over time, on her own, she came to realize the falsehood of polytheism and idolatry prominent in ancient Egypt. Within her own soul stirred the awakening of a revelation of the One God. Willing to forsake all comfort, all honor, all pretenses for the truth of this revelation, she sought to free herself and also her country from the influence of idolatry.

Her father, the Pharaoh, issued the decree requiring that all Jewish male children be killed at birth, attempting to prevent the prediction of a Jewish male redeeming the Jewish people. She defied him. Not only did Batya rescue from the Nile the child who would be the redeemer, she raised him as a prince of Egypt. Without Batya, would there have been a Moses?

A spiritual warrior, Batya sought to transform the entire Egyptian empire from within its own palace. Batya knew from Divine inspiration that the much awaited Jewish redeemer would be raised through her (Midrash HaGadol). She courageously accepted this responsibility. Every morning and evening, Batya would bathe in the cool waters of the Nile River to ease her discomfort from a horrible skin affliction common to the Egyptians. While she was there, she would stroll around, keeping her eyes open for the fulfillment of her prophecy. One day she saw a basket carrying a male Hebrew child in the bulrushes.

There is a legend that Batya's arm miraculously extended to become long enough to reach the basket in the river. It has been said in the merit of Batya, "Stretch your arm and God will do the rest" (Sotah 12b).

When Batya saw this child, she knew that he was the one for whom she was waiting. Not only because there was a spiritual radiance to this child, but legend says that when she touched the basket containing this infant, the boils and scabs all over her body immediately vanished. She was miraculously cured. The

Egyptian sorcerers had forecasted the redeemer of the Jewish people would perish in the water. After Batya had rescued Moses from the water, they no longer saw the sign and the decree was cancelled.

Batya named the child Moses from the word *masha,* "to draw something from water." It should have been *mashuy,* meaning "drawn" in the past tense, as he was drawn out of the water. Batya, however, knew that Moses would "draw" the Jewish people out of Egypt so Batya named him in the present tense of the verb. There were many different names for Moses by his family members. But the Bible only cites the name given to him by Pharaoh's daughter.

The name Batya means "daughter of God." The Talmud records God saying to Pharaoh's daughter, "Although Moses was not your son, you raised him as your very own. I will make you my daughter. You shall be known as Batya, 'God's daughter.'" Her reward was that she was allowed to enter Paradise while she was still alive.

She raised her sons, Moses and Ikhanaton, with the belief in One God. Moses was twenty-six years old when Pharaoh died. Ikhanaton, who had been raised with Moses as a child, known as Amenhotep IV, became the next Pharaoh. Moses was eighteen years old when he left the palace and was out of Egypt during the reign of Ikhanaton. When Moses returned, the Pharaoh was Horemheb, who was not of royal birth. An Egyptian general, Horemheb overthrew Ikhanaton's successor and abolished the cult of Aton, established by Ikhanaton. Even though she was the firstborn of Pharaoh, Batya was spared during the plague that killed the firstborn of Egypt, and she left with the Jewish people as they exited her homeland.

INTERVIEW WITH BATYA

What is your message to our readers?

Batya: It is my prayer and my blessing that every woman and man discover within themselves the unique role that each may play in revealing the Divine in their own lives and in the lives of others. When a man and woman choose to live purposefully and meaningfully, he or she will be protected and supported in the most miraculous of ways. I encourage all to live wisely. Live courageously. Live outrageously, and dedicate your life to the noble purpose your Creator instilled within you.

Please share about your journey to the awakening of your life's purpose.

Batya: Early on, even as a child, I recognized that I was raised as the daughter of Pharaoh not for a life of privilege but for one of responsibility. It would have been quite easy for me to live a life of luxury and riches, but that would not be the truth of who I was and what I came into this world to accomplish. I always knew that I had an important task to accomplish and did not know exactly what it was. I prayed each day that it would become clear to me and that I would be worthy of fulfilling what I came to earth to do.

Through my initiation and training in Egyptian magic and sorcery, I developed certain powers and abilities to manipulate the forces of reality for desired outcomes. Yet with all my knowledge and skill, the deeper yearnings within my soul were not satisfied. Even though I was a princess, I experienced myself as a stranger in my own culture. All the honor and the riches that were given to me because of the position I occupied seemed meaningless and empty to me because they were not based in the deeper truth of reality. Only the truth was important to me. Idolatry became hollow.

You lived in the most polytheistic and richest culture in the world at that time. Your father was considered a god and you were considered a goddess. How did you come to discard that and embrace monotheism?
Batya: Every morning when I would bathe in the Nile, I would immerse myself fully in its cooling waters with the prayer that I be cleansed of all impurity and idolatry. I prayed that I be worthy of receiving the grace of a direct revelation of the One God along with the courage and strength to fulfill the will of the Only One, the True Reality. Through this simple practice, all that I needed to know was revealed to me. This spiritual practice that I later came to know as *mikvah* is a practice that I would like to recommend for everyone.

Would you speak about mikvah? What is it and how did it help you fulfill your purpose? Can it help us too?
Batya: Mikvah, a ritual bath, is a most powerful practice of purification and soul empowerment. Mikvah is the practice of immersion in a natural body of water with intention and purpose. In your time there are special facilities that are built to contain rain water. I used the Nile. It is fine to use any lake, river, or even the ocean. It is customary for a woman to go to mikvah to prepare herself for sexual relations. It is also done to convert a person to become a Jew. I knew all of this intuitively, for the Holy One graciously reveals knowledge to all who sincerely desire to know and serve all of creation.

Mikvah purifies a person on the level of thought, heart, and action. When people think, feel, and act in ways that are self-serving, and not in accordance with Divine Will, they become energetically blocked, unable to receive information from the higher realms. Mikvah cleanses them, renews, and offers them a new start in life. Mikvah is marvelously simple. That's what I like about it.

How did you have the courage to rescue a Hebrew male child when your father ordered them to be murdered?

Batya: I always prayed to live a life of truth, purity, and integrity, even if it was in conflict with everything I had known before. Living a meaningful and purposeful life was always my greatest goal. I knew that such a life offered me the greatest riches, more than all the gold that I had in the palace. External riches were temporary in my eyes, only valuable to the extent that they served this greater truth. When my consciousness was finally awakened to behold the majesty of the One God, the Creator of all of life, I was wholeheartedly dedicated to living from this deeper truth and transmitting it to others. That depth of commitment brought with it courage and faith.

When my father became so obsessed with fear that he was willing to murder innocent male infants to protect himself, I hated him for being so self-serving. He was unworthy of being Pharaoh, ruler of the greatest land in the world.

If he was a god, why did he fear a child? Once again, all too clearly, I saw the emptiness of idolatry for it surely did not provide my father with the courage needed to rule and care beneficently for his people as a leader must. My father wasn't necessarily an evil man, but a fearful, pathetic one. His advisors had knowledge but lacked truth.

I vowed that I would not follow in the path of my father. I would change Egyptian society from within, slowly and gently. I could not be a part of the perpetuation of evil that I witnessed all around me.

How did you plan to affect change in Egypt?

Batya: As a woman, it was not my way to fight, but to wait to be guided by the Holy One for whom all life emanates and all change comes. I prayed deeply and I trusted that my life would be used as an instrument for the greater Divine plan. Much before I discovered Moses, it was revealed to me in meditation that I would raise as my own son the Hebrew child designated to be the redeemer. Together we would redeem both the Jewish people from slavery and cleanse Egypt of idolatry to make it a holy kingdom in the eyes of the Creator.

I intuitively knew that I would educate and train this child for this role that he was designated to perform by the Holy One. As his mother, I would transmit to him the secrets to the deepest mysteries and knowledge that I had been privileged to receive. I trained all my children in the belief of the One God.

My other son, Ikhanaton, who succeeded my father as Pharaoh, established the religion of Aton, the belief in One God for all of Egypt. During his reign, Egypt was purified and became more spiritually refined, until the reign of my beloved son was overthrown by an evil man who sought power for himself.

How did you recognize this particular child, Moses, when you named him as the redeemer?

Batya: It was easy and clear as it came directly from the Creator of the universe. When one day I beheld the shining countenance of an infant in the water, I hoped that this child was the one for whom I long awaited. When I touched the basket that carried him in the water and was healed from this dreadful skin affliction, I knew for certain that I had indeed found my precious son.

The Divine plan that had been transmitted to me in my meditation was now to be actualized. This infant was also so radiant and beautiful. I loved him instantly. I arranged to have him nursed by his biological mother so he would receive the foundation of love and support by her. After his weaning, he would be returned to me and I would raise him as my son.

Why do you feel it was important for Moses to be raised as an Egyptian?

Batya: I knew that it was part of the Divine plan that the redeemer of the Jewish people be raised in the palace. Here he would not only learn and acquire mastery of all that Egyptian magic and occult had to offer, but he would be trained to be a royal leader, a prince of Egypt.

He would not have a slave mentality, fearful and ashamed. Rather he would be strong, confident, and fearless. I personally taught him about how to summon the angelic forces to connect with the One God and receive guidance and knowledge. I always reminded him that he was a Jew and that he had an important role and responsibility to the Jewish people, to me, and to the Holy One. It was our secret.

What is your understanding of what happened in Egypt when you and Moses lived?

Batya: When the Jewish people entered into Egypt, the Divine Presence was with them. I saw this clearly in my meditation. Their presence in the land of Egypt brought blessing to Egypt. It was revealed to me that the Jewish people came into Egypt because it was the will of the Creator. It did not happen by chance, or even by the conscious choosing of the Jewish people.

They thought they were coming to Egypt for food, but rather it was to feed Egypt spiritually. That is the real reason that they came. In the infinite mercy of the Holy One, when the Jewish people were in our land, Egypt was given a chance to attach herself to the Holy One and reject the path of the evil serpent. You might recall Egypt's fascination with serpents. Men even shaved their heads to better resemble the snake. The magicians of Egypt had gained tremendous spiritual power through the manipulation of the demonic forces. We used divination. We communed with the spirits of the deceased. We consulted ghosts and disembodied entities. We were master sorcerers and astrologers.

Over time, I, along with many others, realized that the power of Egypt was sourced in impurity and fear and not in faith or connection with the source of truth and goodness. I did all I could to educate and spread the belief in One God among Egyptians. When it became clear that Egypt could not change from within, for evil had permeated its very fiber, many Egyptians, the best of Egypt, chose to leave Egypt with the Jewish people and follow Moses and the path of faith that he taught.

This act took great courage. Ultimately, those Egyptians who left assimilated into the Jewish people, forgetting that they were once Egyptians. Many of them were once the master sorcerers and magicians, the elite of Egypt.

Do you have any final words for people living today?

Batya: I am sad to announce to people in your time that the power of the serpent still lives. It may not be clear to modern people today who and what the serpent is. In your time know that the serpent is the power of illusion and of falsehood.

First, to combat the evil of the serpent, you must know that the serpent thrives on fear. It becomes more powerful when you are afraid. Do not be afraid. It has no real power except what you give it. So do not let fear stop you.

Today, as in my time, each person must choose to follow the path of the truth and goodness. Reject the serpent whose life force energy is based on what is unreal and false. When enough people give up their inner truth, because they are frightened, the power of evil increases. But when people are connected to the truth, the power of the serpent is vanquished.

What should people do?

Batya: Firstly, attach yourself to the Creator of life and you are unstoppable. There is no obstacle that you cannot overcome. Live your life with confidence and joy. Be willing to break out of your comfort zone. Your true self, who you really are, is deeper and more powerful than your fear-based ego self. Remember, you came into this life for a purpose. It is not to accumulate wealth that you cannot take with you when you leave your physical body.

To discover what this purpose is for you, each of you must also go "out of Egypt," that place of bondage; depart from the belief in what is false to walk in what is truth with faith.

Until you make this exodus for yourself with the help of the Divine, you will find yourself in bondage. May you be blessed to bring yourself and help bring others from darkness to light, from bondage to freedom.

CONCLUDING RESPONSE TO MOTHER BATYA

(It is suggested that this be read out loud by the reader or group).

> *Mother Batya, you are such an inspiration to us. You were truly worthy of being the mother of Moses, the redeemer of the Jewish people. You model to us a person who was courageous enough to trust her inner knowing and act upon it. We want to be more like you. We want to have your courage. We will listen and honor what is revealed to us in the deep recesses of our soul like you did.*

> *Too often we betray our own inner knowing to please other people. We seek to be comfortable rather than authentic. We play it safe, rather than speak and act in ways that honor God and what we know as the truth in our heart and soul. Admittedly, we have been selfish, shortsighted and impatient. With you as our example, we affirm right now that we will live more courageously and selflessly.*

> *Only by being selfless and courageous like you were will we know the true vitality of life. Our life is a Divine gift that we treasure. In this very moment, we make a deep choice to devote ourselves more wholeheartedly to the discovery of our holy purpose for being created on the earth at this time. We affirm now that we do trust ourselves to live more fully from our deep inner knowing. We affirm that we will honor the Divine Presence in all that we are and do.*

PRAYER TO THE GOD OF MOTHER BATYA

> *May the God of Mother Batya empower me to live the truth that is revealed within my own soul no matter what the environment dictates I should do and who I should be.*

What Quality of the Feminine Does Batya Demonstrate?

Batya demonstrates the courage and power of a woman in touch with the feminine to trust inner knowing, and not be defined by externalities. The Egyptians worshipped the Nile as a god. Batya in her feminine wisdom realized the falsehood of this idolatry. She chose to not give away her inner power and inner knowing as a woman to serve what was false.

She defied her father, the Pharaoh. When she saw the basket containing Moses in the water, she had compassion, totally aware that it probably contained one of the Hebrew male infants that her father wanted killed. She raised this son as her own, right in the palace of her father. She left Egypt with the Jewish people.

What Spiritual Practice Do We Learn from Batya?
The Spiritual Practice of Mikvah

In the body of the interview, Batya speaks about the spiritual practice of mikvah. Mikvah is the immersion in a natural body of water for purposes of purification. Most Jewish communities maintain a public mikvah that may be used. An ocean, river, or lake is also acceptable. Mikvah is done by a woman to resume sexual relations after menstruation and to convert a person to Judaism. Mikvah is also done for spiritual purposes, to release negativity and open oneself to greater revelation of Godliness.

MIKVAH MEDITATION

To be done solely as a meditation or as preparation for actual mikvah experience.

When you go to mikvah or a body of water for the purposes of immersion, prior to immersion, make a strong intention that by this act, or through this meditation, you will indeed be cleansed and purified. Your intention is always important. In your imagination or in actuality prior to a real mikvah experience, remove all your garments. In addition to disrobing, let go of all the roles you have to play in your life. Take a few moments to meditate. You are not what you do. You are not the roles you play.

Experience yourself as totally naked, deeply alone, and gloriously vulnerable. Allow the deep inward yearning to be whole, to be pure, to simply become stronger as you prepare for immersion. When you finally enter into the water—in actuality or in your imagination—let the water surround your entire body. When you are in the mikvah, it is like you are returning to the womb. Imagine that now you are on the inside of God. The walls of separation are removed between you and God. The love, compassion, and strength of the Creator of the universe surrounds you, embraces you, and permeates you.

Open to Divine love. You are unconditionally loved for that is the nature of love of the Creator. You are loved for simply being you. Open to this feeling, affirm it, and know it as a primary truth.

When you are under the water, this is the most auspicious time to ask for what you want. Immerse yourself several times in the mikvah, take note of the experience of being fully immersed in the water, and then prepare to leave the mikvah and take a moment to be with any openings that occurred through this experience or visualization.

KEY QUESTIONS FOR REFLECTION AND FOLLOW-UP DISCUSSION ON BATYA

1. Do you think that Batya has been sufficiently appreciated in Judaism and Christianity? Without Batya, would there have been a Moses?
2. How might we call greater attention to the important role that she played?
3. Batya demonstrated the power of the feminine to both discern and remain faithful to her inner truth. In the midst of an idolatrous country, she was a Jew.
4. How is Batya a meaningful model for you in your personal life?

CHAPTER EIGHT

CHANA'S PRAYER
SECRETS OF GETTING PRAYERS ANSWERED

Do not be afraid to make yourself vulnerable before God. You cannot do life on your own. When you stand before God in prayer, it is essential that you be authentic. God is close to all who call sincerely from the heart. When your heart is open, you will experience God and know firsthand that your words make a difference. God loves you more than you can fathom.

—Chana

CHANA
MOTHER AND PROPHETESS

Chana, esteemed as one of the seven ancient prophetesses, is regarded as the role model for prayer for both men and women for all times. The Jewish guidelines and laws of prayer are formulated from her. Each *Rosh Hashanah*, one of the holiest days in the Jewish calendar, the story of Chana and her prophetic song are read. Not only because her prayers to bear a son were answered on that day, but also because her words and her life story itself inspire us to call out in prayer more powerfully and authentically on this most auspicious day of blessing.

Many women like Chana throughout the ages have been challenged with infertility. Even biblical women like Sarah, Rebecca, Rachel, and Miriam prayed as they each confronted this challenge. Chana's challenge of infertility is recorded in depth in the Bible, not just for the particular child she bore out of her prayer, but because the way in which she prayed for this son was unique. No one had ever prayed like this before.

As with biblical women before her, Chana's prayers for a child were not answered immediately. When Chana had been infertile for more than ten years of marriage, her husband Elkanah, at Chana's suggestion, married a second wife, Peninah, who quickly bore him ten sons in eight years. Rather than being grateful to Chana, Peninah ridiculed her for her barrenness.

Chana lived in the time period before the Holy Temple in Jerusalem was built. At the time, it was customary to journey to Shiloh to make sacrificial offerings where the tabernacle that held the Shechinah was maintained. Chana would journey with her husband annually to pray for a child there. It was in Shiloh that Chana's prayers were finally answered. Upon witnessing one of her prayer sessions, Eli the Prophet first accused her of being drunk because she moved her lips in her pleading with God. Apparently, Chana was praying in a way that was not commonly done before. To this very day, however, people emulate Chana in their prayer by moving their lips and speaking in a whisper. Chana is also credited with revealing for the first time in her prayer the Divine Name of *Adonai Tzva'ot,* Lord of Hosts.

When Chana finally offered her child to God and said, "God, Master of Legions, if You do not forget your maidservant and You remember me and give

Your maidservant male offspring, then I shall give him to God all the days of his life" (1 Sam. 1:11), her prayers were answered.

When Samuel, her son, finished nursing, Chana brought him to Eli to raise and teach him to be a prophet. As she surrendered her beloved child, Chana joyously uttered a most profound and awesome song that transmitted the highest spiritual teachings and prophecies for the future. Through this song, it is clear that Chana personally attained the most elevated consciousness of the Divine. There are many songs that have been recorded in the Bible. Miriam sings at the Red Sea, Devorah sings before battle, Moses also sings, but Chana's song is considered the highest praise, beyond any song or praise ever uttered by a man or woman before.

We know from her song that Chana knew prophetically that her son Samuel would be the principal prophet in the land of Israel in the days when Israel would be miraculously saved from the Philistines. Samuel indeed became one of the primary Jewish prophets for all times, even compared in stature to the prophecy of Moses. He ruled as a prophet in Israel for ten years on his own, then for two years with Saul, and seven years with David in Hebron.

In the book of Samuel, Chana's song is recorded. It is written, "A barren woman bore seven" (1 Sam. 2:5). This prophecy was literally fulfilled. After bearing Samuel, Chana was blessed to birth five more sons. Chana lived to see the two sons of Samuel and these two grandsons were considered like sons for her. It is also said in the oral tradition that when Chana would birth a son, Peninah would bury two sons. When Peninah had already buried eight sons, and Chana was expecting her fifth son, Peninah went to Chana and said the following., "I know that I have sinned against you. Please forgive me so that my two sons I have left will live." Chana prayed for them. (Peseta Rabbasi 44:7) They lived and were also considered as sons of Chana.

INTERVIEW WITH CHANA

It is such an honor to be with you today. Do you have a message for people today?

Chana: Prayer is potent. Even though your prayers may not be answered quickly, never give up. Every person has something important to bring into this world. You must pray unceasingly to be capable of fulfilling what you came into this world to do. The loftier your soul mission is, the greater the challenges you will confront. If you feel guided to bring forth something positive in the world, you must pray continually, do all that you can, and have faith that your prayers will be answered. Do not give up.

As we look at your life, we witness the power of prayer. Yet, why was it necessary for you to suffer so much before your prayers were finally answered?

The deeper underlying question is, "Why do good people like you, and like so many of our readers, have to suffer?" Do you have a message for them?

Chana: On one hand, it is really heartbreaking that people have to suffer in this world, but please know that suffering is the primary means by which a person is refined and cleansed. Suffering is actually a Divine gift of love, offering an opportunity to come closer to the Holy One that enables a person to grow spiritually.

There are all kinds of challenges. Every person will endure pain and suffering at some time in life. Some people will have health challenges; some people will have financial challenges; others will have love challenges. Ultimately, all pain and suffering is a blessing. How a person suffers holds the keys to the particular soul correction needed for them to fulfill their soul mission. Most people complain to others about suffering rather than cry out to the Only One who can transform their suffering into blessing. Suffering becomes a gift when it is a springboard for prayer.

If you are strong, have faith, determination, and maintain your focus, you will be victorious and reap the spiritual rewards from your toil and tribulation. In time, you will be grateful for the challenges you have been Divinely given, for they have been the fertile soil upon which access to your own holy soul deepened and grew.

How does this important teaching apply in your life?

Chana: When I saw that God had closed my womb and did not allow me to bear children, I knew that I had to pray for a child from the depths of my heart. When my prayers were still not answered, I told my husband to take another wife. Perhaps I could have children through her like Rachel and Leah had children through their handmaidens. And so it was that Peninah, the second wife, was blessed with children easily while I remained barren. But Peninah and I were not sisters or friends as I had hoped we would be. She was unwilling to allow me to play any role in her children's lives. She lauded being a mother over me all the time and continually taunted me for not having children.

She would rise early and taunt me, "Aren't you going to get up and wash your children's faces so they can go to school?" and continue throughout each day with these kinds of insensitive remarks. Her cruelty made my plight of childlessness even more painful but it also made me even more determined than ever to storm the gates of heaven with prayer.

What do you mean by storming the gates of heaven?
Chana: I did not pray quietly for a child nor did I surrender gracefully to my fate. Rather, I channeled the negative emotions of anger, bitterness, and even jealousy that I was experiencing to strengthen and deepen my connection with the Holy One. I not only supplicated myself before God, I debated God. I bargained with God and I even demanded that God give me what I wanted. I was bold and audacious in prayer and in life. I never stopped praying because in my heart of hearts I knew that God loved me. I knew that it would just be a matter of time before my prayers would be answered.

What do you mean by being bold in prayer? Can you give some examples?
Chana: I challenged God and declared, "Nothing that you create is superfluous. So what are my breasts that You placed on my heart if not for nursing? Give me a son!" (*Berachos* 31b).

I channeled the negative emotions of anger and even threatened to play the adulterous woman. When a woman in my time was suspected of adultery, she would be brought to the priests and ordered to drink a special potion. If she was guilty, she would die instantly a painful death. If she was innocent, she would be blessed with a child. I continued with so many arguments. I did not relent.

When I finally made a "deal" with God, that I would give my son to Eli to raise as his own, my prayers were answered. I named my son Samuel, which means "I have requested him from God."

Why do you feel your prayers were finally answered?
Chana: I believe that my prayers were finally answered when I became sufficiently cleansed, purified, and spiritually worthy of bearing such a holy son. This child would be a savior for God's holy people. Through my soul wrestling, inner work, and deep prayer, I grew in my understanding of what it is to be a true mother. To be a mother is such a privilege.

The truth was that I was angry with God because I had not experienced being a mother. My anger caused within me a sense of feeling separate from God. Feeling separate and abandoned by God is very painful. In my heart of hearts, I came to know that it was the closeness with God that I deeply desired, more than anything in the world. I realized that my desire for this child was not for my personal glorification, but rather it was a way of my coming close to God.

When I was able to make the most supreme gift of offering this son to God, only then were my prayers answered. To be worthy of bearing this child, I had to surrender him to God. This was God's plan from the beginning. This child was holy! There was a golden light that surrounded him and seemed to emanate and radiate from him. When I gave my son to Eli to be raised as a prophet, I experienced a closeness with God much greater than I had ever experienced before. After birthing this extraordinary child, I was truly fulfilled.

This particular child was the answer to my prayers. The love and training he would receive from Eli would enable him to fulfill his soul mission better than I could ever have done. After the birth of Samuel, I was even blessed with additional children. God is awesome and generous.

How did you have the strength to keep on praying for so many years?

Chana: From my prayer and meditation, it had been revealed to me that I was destined to give birth to a prophet who would guide and save the Jewish people. I had reason to keep praying. Because my son was such a lofty soul, I understood that it would be very hard for me to bear him. As long as I had breath in my body, I would never give up praying for this particular son.

Do you have any guidance for others about prayer?

Chana: Never give up! Never give up! Throughout my entire life, I never gave up praying for this son. My husband would try to comfort me by telling me that he loved me more than ten sons. He so much wanted me to be happy with my lot, but I would not be appeased. I would not give up.

How does a person begin to pray?

Chana: Speak to God the words of your heart and soul. Be real and be authentic. Do not waste time praying for what is superficial, but pray only for what you need from the core of your soul.

It is important to ascertain that what you want must be attuned to what you would imagine God would want for you as well. For example, my soul told me to keep praying, because God wanted this child to be born. When you do this, you are not simply praying for yourself, but also for God. At the root and core of your personal prayers must be the prayer for a greater revelation of Godliness in this world.

After personal reflection, then open your mouth, and speak out loud from the depths of your heart, yet also allow the words to flow through you. Make your case, present your arguments, and convince God of the worthiness of your prayers. It is good to even debate God like I did. Most importantly, tell God how you will be able to love and serve more if your prayers are fulfilled.

Do you have particular advice for people whose prayers are not answered quickly?

Chana: Remember this: people are often deprived of what they want because God wants their prayers to help them forge a deeper bond with Him. For example, the snake in the Garden of Eden story was cursed to eat dust. At first glance, it looks like the snake was blessed because everything he needed was readily available for him. The truth is that this was a curse because he did not have to pray for what he needed. Recognizing your need for prayer is a spiritual gift and an opportunity when and if the challenges you are confronting energize your prayer life.

When you know directly that you need God, you cannot live the life you want on your own, you are indeed blessed. It is the lack, the deficiency that you are experiencing, that actually helps to forge a more dynamic and meaningful bond with God. You grow through challenge in ways that are not possible any other way. Because you do not at the time have the whole picture you are unable to appreciate the blessing that is contained within the challenge you are confronting.

Can you offer us some tips to make our prayers more effective?

Chana: With delight. I went through so much, so I have something to teach others regarding prayer. I want to reveal an important secret to having your prayers answered.

Whenever you pray for something in particular, be sure to include in your meditation and prayers your personal yearning for closeness with God. Always take time to express your gratitude for all the blessings in your life. Gratitude opens the gates of blessing and answering prayers. If it is difficult for you to be thankful because you are angry or hurt, it is also good for you to express those feelings as well. God wants your heart, so be real and honest.

If your prayers are not answered immediately, as mine were not, and yet you continue to pour out your heart to God like I did, not recoiling in anger or surrendering in defeat, you will ultimately be victorious. By your faith and the sincere intensity of your prayer, you will draw down infinite blessings and a profound inner joy to you, whether your prayers for something specific are answered or not. The greatest gift that you will receive from prayer is the deepening of your relationship with God.

Would you please further instruct us on how to pray? Are there any more secrets?

Chana: I'd like to share a few more secrets for having your prayers answered.

Even though you may be praying for your own needs, be sure to also pray for others as well. Most importantly, pray for the Jewish people, and pray for peace in Jerusalem. If you do this, you will be more greatly blessed even more than if you pray just for your own welfare or benefit. People who pray for the Jewish people and for Jerusalem even gain a spiritual radiance that makes them shine for all the world to see.

God is the ultimate giver, so to be close to God is to become a giver in your life. Seek opportunities to give to others and to God alone. It may be a little secret, but whenever you make a sincere offering to God, to do something for God, God rewards you beyond your wildest hopes and dreams. You must however be careful that your giving is not simply a way to bribe God. Give as a way to become closer to God. By giving you will naturally become a greater vessel worthy of receiving additional blessings in your life. When we are willing to truly give something of ourselves, we become more worthy.

When I expressed my willingness to give my beloved son to Eli the Prophet to raise as his spiritual son, my prayers to have a son were quickly answered. Not only did my son become an awesome prophet, but I was also personally rewarded with a profound revelation of God.

Thousands of women and men recite the words of my song to this very day and the song lifts them up to the highest levels of consciousness. What a gift this revelation was for me and also to the world. I have been greatly blessed. That is how the Divine works. Whenever we give to others and to God, we are blessed. Look always for opportunities to give to others.

If prayer is so wonderful, why do people stop praying?

Chana: Many people envision God as a sugar daddy who will fulfill their hopes and dreams. In the act of prayer, they attempt to bargain or bribe God to have their hopes and wishes fulfilled. If God does not respond accordingly in the time period that they deem appropriate, these people often stop praying. If life is harsh, they also stop praying.

It would appear from their rejection of God that they want God only on their terms. If they do not get what they want, when they want it, they become angry with God. They may cry that God has abandoned or rejected them, but it is they who have abandoned and rejected God. It is they who terminate a relationship with God, not God. This is most unfortunate. They do not realize that the Holy One, by not answering their prayers, has given them an even greater opportunity to grow, to be cleansed and purified and become a better person. God always does good. It is we who must lift up our eyes and heart to see the blessings even in the challenges we confront, and grow from them.

It is so important that a person not give up and continue to turn to God daily in prayer. It is principally through prayer that a person grows and is transformed. Do not be afraid to make yourself vulnerable before God. You cannot do life on your own. When you stand before God in prayer, it is essential that you be authentic. God is close to all who call sincerely, from the heart. When your heart is open, you will experience God and know firsthand that your words will make a difference. God loves you more than you can fathom.

Thank you. I have come to understand now that it is the relationship with God established through prayer that is even more important than having one's prayers answered. I would like to conclude our interview with reciting your most beautiful song for our readers and ask you to comment on it. Here it is, as written in our holy books:

My heart rejoices in God, my glory is raised by God, my mouth derides my enemies because I rejoice in your salvation.

Do not talk so very proudly, let not arrogance come from your mouth. For God is a Lord of knowledge and by him actions are weighed.

The bows of the mighty men are broken, while those who stumbled are girded with strength.

Those who had plenty have hired themselves out for bread, while those who were hungry are at ease. The barren has borne seven and she who had many children is desolate.

God causes death and brings to life. God brings down to the grave and raises up.

God makes poor and makes rich. God brings low and lifts up.

God lifts the poor from the dust and raises the beggar from the rubbish, to be seated among princes and inherit a seat of honor. For the pillars of the earth are God's and God has set the world on them.

God will guard the feet of his saints and the wicked will perish in darkness, for no man will prevail by strength.

> *God's foes will be crushed. God will thunder in heaven against them. God will judge the ends of the earth. God will give strength to his king and exalt the power of his anointed.*

Chana: Recite my song each day, study the verses, internalize them into your heart, and you will be transformed. Everything that I know about life is contained within these words.

Do you have any further concluding words for men and women?
Chana: Always talk to God in your own words each day. Express your honest and deepest feelings to the Holy One, the Only One, who can help you, heal you, and answer your prayers. Be strong in faith. Never give up. This is my blessing to all.

PRAYER TO THE GOD OF MOTHER CHANA
(It is suggested that this be read out loud by the reader or group.)

> *May the God of Mother Chana empower me to pray unceasingly for my needs, for the needs of others, for the welfare of the Jewish people, and the peace of Jerusalem. May I never give up praying for what is good and what I truly need to fulfill my soul purpose. May I be strong, courageous, and grow through prayer.*

What Quality of the Feminine Does Chana Demonstrate?
The Jewish oral tradition recorded in the body of knowledge known as the "Gemara" tells us that women have been given the gift of speech. We only have to look around us to easily note that women generally like to talk more than men. Heart-centered communication is also more important to women because women are more attuned to their emotions and feel more deeply. Therefore, we are told that when a woman directs her heartfelt words in prayer to God, she can truly bring down blessings. A man must similarly access the feminine within him to draw down blessings as well.

Women are generally more internal and find their connection to God internally more than externally. Wherever a woman prays, God is present. A woman is a priestess with a direct connection to the Divine. Though a woman may enjoy communal prayer services and participate in them, there is no Jewish spiritual obligation as there is for a man. According to Jewish law, a woman is not obligated to attend synagogue or pray communally except for a few days in a year. Individual prayer such as talking to God in her own words, meditation, and heartfelt sharing in intimate women's circles may be more powerful for women than traditional services. Men need to be obligated for public worship as a way to bond with other men. A woman does not need to be required to bond with others. She will naturally bond with other women because that is her nature to do so.

What Meditative and Spiritual Practice Do We Learn from Chana?
The Spiritual Practice of Prayer

Chana boldly opens the gates of prayer for all people in a new way. Because of Chana, people are encouraged to talk to God authentically, debate, and even argue with God if necessary to have their prayers answered. Chana also demonstrated vulnerability as well as fortitude and strength in her prayer life. She prayed as a woman and models to men and women a new way to pray.

A person is advised to talk directly to God in one's own words every day. Many great teachers in the Jewish tradition like Rabbi Nachman of Breslov advocated the simple and powerful practice of talking out loud to God each day. During this time period, a person should feel free to pour out their hearts to God, express all the pain, troubles, regrets, needs, and desires as well as make requests. If necessary, a person should scream and shout either aloud or silently. Upon completion of this type of prayer, a person should trust that the prayers of the heart uttered have been heard.

KEY QUESTIONS AND FOLLOW-UP DISCUSSION ON CHANA

1. Do you think it is right or best to pray specifically for something you want and argue like Chana did, as opposed to praying for acceptance of Divine Will? Is one approach better than the other?
2. Doesn't God know what we want? Why should we pray for something specific? If it was Divine Will that we should have something, would we not have it? Is it not higher to attune ourselves to Divine Will and accept our lot in life with gratitude?
3. Why do we have to pray? How is prayer more than our personal and collective shopping bag of requests?
4. When you pray, do you include requests for your personal needs?
5. When have you ever cried, argued, and even debated God like Chana? How did that make you feel about God, especially when your prayers were not answered the way you wanted them to be? Or perhaps they were answered, and your life became even more difficult. Have you ever been angry with God?

6. What about the role of personal responsibility in creating the life that you want? Should we have to pray for what we can do ourselves or should we take responsibility to do what we can do to make what we want happen in our lives? How do you reconcile personal responsibility with Divine Will?

CHAPTER NINE

QUEEN ESTHER
THE SECRET OF HER POWER AND BEAUTY

Giving creates bonding. It is important for Jews and all people in the world to give to others, for no other reason than to express love and unity with them. Every person must overcome the selfish desire to receive for oneself alone by sharing with others. Only by sharing and giving to others can one draw blessings to the world.

—*Queen Esther*

ESTHER
PROPHETESS AND SAVIOR OF THE JEWISH PEOPLE

Esther, one of the seven prophetesses within Judaism, was also considered to be one of the four most beautiful women who have ever lived. Sarah, Avigail, and Rachav are the other most beautiful women cited in the Talmud.

Esther lived in Persia (now Iran) in the time period after the destruction of the first Holy Temple in Jerusalem. Along with her uncle/husband Mordecai, Esther is accredited for saving the Jewish people living in the one –hundred – twenty-seven provinces ruled by Persia at the time. An annual community reading of her book, the Megillah of Esther, a retelling of the story of her life and the events surrounding the miracle that occurred in her time, is considered mandatory throughout the worldwide Jewish community.

Esther, given the name Hadassah (meaning "myrtle") at birth, was called Esther when she became queen of Persia. The nations of the world called her Istahar, meaning "beautiful like the moon." Her name was also said to be derived from *satar*, in Hebrew meaning "secret," or *histera*, in Hebrew meaning "hidden," because Esther kept her identity secret.

Esther was an orphan. Her father died at the time of her conception and her mother at her birth. She was raised by her uncle Mordecai, though Esther was also said to be the daughter of Mordecai's uncle. There are many who say that Mordecai married her when she was of marriageable age. Her status is unclear. Esther is a mystery.

The Megillah, written by Esther, tells us that, "Esther would find grace in the eyes of all who saw her" (Esther 2:15). Everyone who saw her thought she was a member of his nation (Megillah 13a). It was more than her beauty and unique spiritual radiance that made her so appealing and attractive to everyone she met. She was the exceptional kind of person who mirrored back to others their own beauty.

Seemingly selfless, she didn't need to prove or validate herself through her contact with others, but rather she could seem to be whoever a person wanted her to be. She was exceedingly humble, almost self-effacing, but in the most gracious, elegant, and dignified way. To be in her presence was to feel elevated, validated, and charmed. Esther, actually a descendent of King Saul, was true royalty from the House of Israel. She always knew who she was, but her true identity was hidden from the world.

King Asherverous, a commoner, had seized the throne of the empire of Persia and married Vashti, a Babylonian princess, as a way to legitimize his claim to the throne. When he felt secure enough in his reign, after three years he held a week-long feast to celebrate his reign and invited everyone to attend, even the Jews. When he was drunk enough on one of the nights, he sought to debase his wife by demanding that she dance naked before him and everyone at the party.

"You are worse than the stable boy of my father. He could at least hold his liquor. You can't" (Megillah 12b).

According to the Gemara, this was Vashti's retort to this request. For her insubordination and refusal to follow his commands, King Asherverous had her murdered to demonstrate to all of his subjects that he was independent of her. Because Vashti stood up to her husband, she is celebrated in some feminist circles. According to Jewish teachings, Vashti was, however, known for her arrogance and cruelty, particularly with the young Jewish maidservants who she would make work naked on the Sabbath, knowing that it was against what they believed.

It is said that a person is treated measure for measure. Vashti's refusal to dance naked at the party resulted in her death. Chided on by his advisor Haman, after the death of Vashti, King Asherverous issued a rather ridiculous decree proclaiming throughout all the provinces that every man should be the ruler of his own home.

In his search for a new queen, all girls of a certain age were ordered to appear before the officials for consideration. Eventually Esther was selected to be the queen and was placed in a position where she was able to save the Jewish people from an edict calling for their annihilation. Much of the story is told in the subsequent interview with her.

Read the Megillah of Esther for the entire story of Esther.

INTERVIEW WITH ESTHER

It is such an honor to be with you. You have been such an inspiration to so many men and women. Would you introduce yourself to our readers and share with us something about your life?

Esther: First, I send my love and blessings to all. The main thing that I want you to know about me is that my life was blessed. It was clear to me that I was where I was supposed to be. I was privileged to be in the position as queen of Persia where I could help save the Jewish people and rebuild the Holy Temple through my son. My life had meaning and purpose so I was happy.

How did you become the queen of Persia, one of the capitals of the world at the time when you lived?

Esther: I was forced to enter a beauty contest after King Asherverous murdered his wife for refusing to dance naked before him and others at a party. They were celebrating the destruction of the Holy Temple in Jerusalem. Soon after that, the king began looking for a replacement wife. All girls of a certain age were ordered to appear before the government officials for consideration.

After I was selected to be one of the girls who would appear before the king for the final selection by him personally, I had to undergo a year of beauty preparation, six months soaking with the oil of myrrh and six months with perfumes and cosmetics. I had no desire to marry this evil man, but it would appear that my being queen was part of the Divine plan as I learned much later.

I hadn't requested anything special to beautify myself as all the other girls had done prior to their appearance before the king. Nevertheless, when he saw me, he placed the royal crown on my head.

You said earlier that your life was blessed. But what about your personal happiness? You had to stay married to King Asherverous for the rest of your life. There are even some people who say that you were married to Mordecai when you were kidnapped by the king and forced to enter the beauty contest. If that was true, how much more difficult it must have been for you to stay married to the king, knowing that your beloved one was so close by but you could no longer be together with him as a married couple. No one talks enough about this tremendous sacrifice that you made to save the Jewish people.

Esther: I learned very early in my life to accept life and Divine Will graciously. Because my parents died before I was born, I grew up very aware of the spiritual world. As I did not know my parents physically, they were not limited physically to me. As far back as I can remember, I always felt enveloped with their love and God's love as well.

My life was never limited to the physical sphere. When I lived in a body known as Esther, I accepted life as it was, because I experienced whatever was happening in life as an expression of Divine Will. My life was not easy nor was Mordecai's, but together and individually we surrendered to what was and always sought to align ourselves with the Holy One's will.

Knowing that there was no other choice for me, I understood that it was Divine Will that I stay married to this king. Over time, I grew in compassion for the king and that helped to refine and uplift him. Being queen of a large empire also provided me with the privilege of caring for so many people, Jews and non-Jews. I am grateful for the opportunities given to me to serve and give. And of course my son Darius was my joy, my hope, and inspiration.

Please tell us more about the circumstances that resulted in the holiday of Purim. What was your role in helping to save the Jewish people?

Esther: When Mordecai refused to bow to Haman, Haman convinced the king to issue an order calling for the extermination of the Jewish people on a particular day in the month of Adar. The Jewish people were such a small minority within the empire, yet we were perceived as a threat. The king was all too happy to eliminate the Jewish people because he also feared their spiritual power.

Though this evil decree was a secret, Mordecai overheard a few guards discussing it. He quickly informed me of this decree and challenged me to plead for the welfare of the Jewish people before the king. I was initially resistant, because to appear before the king uninvited had previously meant death to anyone who tried.

Before this, I had been passive in my relationship with the king. I was distressed that Mordecai was now asking me to initiate a different relationship with the king. I didn't want to do this at all!

Mordecai then reminded me of the most important teaching. I remember his very words to this day. "Do not imagine that you will be able to escape in the king's palace any more than the rest of the Jews. If you persist in keeping silent at a time like this, relief and deliverance will come to the Jewish people from some other place, while you and your father's house will perish. Who knows whether it was just for such a time as this that you attained the royal position" (Megillah 4:13–14).

From his words, I clearly saw that my being in the palace as Queen was part of the Divine plan. I was in this position because I had been given the privilege to serve the Jewish people and make a difference. If I did not do what God wanted me to do, someone else would do it instead of me.

What did you then do?

Esther: Because I needed spiritual fortitude to do this, I immediately asked the entire Jewish people in Shushan to pray and fast for me for three days. I intuitively knew that it was only because the Jewish people are divided among ourselves that we have enemies. When the Jewish people are unified, we will be victorious.

The Jewish people at the time must have known this as well, because quite miraculously they were willing to undertake this arduous fast. My maidens and

I also fasted and prayed incessantly for three days. Though the fast may have weakened me physically, it strengthened me spiritually. Because I was unified with the Jewish people, I gained the strength and faith needed to carry out my mission. On the third day of the fast, I received *Ruach Hakodesh,* the Holy Spirit.

What happened next? I'm enthralled.
Esther: To speak to the king, I had to walk down a very long corridor to the king's office. As I walked down the corridor, I was confronted with all the idols of the country that adorned the hall. The palace courtiers tried to intimidate me the whole time with many terrible threats. Even though I was fearful, I kept on walking, finding the faith and trust deep within me that I would be protected and successful in carrying out my mission.

When the king finally saw me, he seemed defenseless. He told me that I appeared to him as an angel and that his soul left him for a moment. He then offered me "up to half of my kingdom, your petition should be granted" (Megillah 5:3). Surely God was at work.

Even though the king was very loving toward me in that moment, I intuitively knew it was not the time to make my request directly to him. My pleading for the Jewish people at that time would not be sufficient. The king would need to see clearly for himself the evil of Haman to rescind his terrible decree. It occurred to me that I simply needed to create doubt in the king's mind about the trustworthiness of Haman.

As a woman I could do that best by inspiring jealousy within the king. I invited the king and Haman to a party. I trusted that the perfect opportunity would present itself at a party for me to reveal my true identity and turn the king against Haman. I recorded all the events in my scroll that is read annually throughout the Jewish world for those who would like more details.

At the first festivity, I placed my couch next to Haman and gave him my goblet, so as to arouse jealousy. It worked. The king saw this and was jealous and annoyed. No opportunity, however, presented itself for me to reveal my true identity at the first party, so I invited the king and Haman to another party the next evening.

I learned at the second party the king had been unable to sleep the night before so he reviewed his records and discovered that Mordecai had done him a great favor that was not rewarded. The next day, he asked Haman what he should do to show favor to someone. Haman described all kinds of wonderful honors, thinking that he was the one the king wanted to favor. How surprised and visibly shaken he was to discover that it was Mordecai and not he who the king wanted to honor.

The king then asked me what I wanted. "What is your request, Queen Esther, it shall be granted to you, even if it be up to half the kingdom" (Megillah 7:2). At this moment, I clearly knew that this was indeed my opening. I seized the moment, revealed my true identity as a Jew, and informed the king that Haman wanted to kill me and my people.

The king quickly rose from the wine fest, and angrily left the room. When he soon returned, he saw Haman prostrated on my couch. It must have looked like Haman was going to assault me. Furious, the king ordered that Haman hang on the very gallows that Haman had prepared to hang Mordecai for failing to bow to him.

What happened then?
Esther: The king gave the estate of Haman to me, and the signet ring that the king had removed from Haman he gave to Mordecai. Mordecai left the king's office in royal apparel with a large gold crown on his head. Though the king was unable to rescind his first decree, he issued an edict that the Jews may defend themselves. There was a war, but the Jews were victorious and celebrated their victory on the fourteenth of Adar. The fighting continued in the walled city of Shushan until the fifteenth of the month, so that became the date of Shushan Purim.

What a story! Everything seemed to be going one way and then it was miraculously turned around. Haman was hung on the very same gallows he'd prepared to hang Mordecai.
Esther: Yes, that is what often happens. Life can change in a moment.

This also seems true for you as well. When you were selected to be Queen, you were said to be a shy and almost self-effacing woman. At the end of your story, you are bold and even telling the sages in Sanhedrin what to do.
Esther: After the war, I petitioned the sages of the Sanhedrin that the scroll I wrote recording the events of my day be read by the Jewish people for eternity in a celebration honoring the miracle of the deliverance of the Jewish people in my time. "Establish my story for all generations" as it says in my scroll (Megillah 7:29). Initially the sages refused me, but I prevailed and my request was approved.

How did you change from being meek to becoming assertive and even bold? Do you have any guidance on how women may be similarly empowered?
Esther: Quite simply, I did what was necessary. I was empowered because there was a need to be met and I was in the best position to meet that need. I also

knew how to use my power as a woman. When I unified my heart with that of the Jewish people during the fast, I was purified and spiritually empowered to carry out this important mission of saving the Jewish people. Any person in my position would have done what I had to do.

Similarly, any woman who becomes aware of the needs of people around her and realizes that she is in the best position to meet these needs will be Divinely empowered. Like me, she must also pray and purify herself so that she receives Divine assistance. We are all conduits of blessing in God's plan. If we do not do what should be done, someone else will do it. Unfortunately, we will then miss out on the privilege of being a blessing.

But, isn't it unusual for a scroll to be written by a woman?
Esther: Yes, that's true. It's unusual for a woman to write a scroll. You must first know that it was not for my personal glory that I recorded these events in a scroll and asked that they be canonized within the holy books of the Jewish people. I did so because there was so much to learn from these events around this story. Most importantly this Purim story has relevance for future times. It was primarily for this reason that I requested that my scroll be read every year.

The fact that deliverance came through me, a woman, is also very significant for the future as well. It will be the women who will help usher in the final redemption. I simply served as a model for what women must do in the future.

When Asherverous first issued that terrible decree against the Jewish people in your time, you did not record any outcry of opposition from the non-Jews. Was there an outcry? If not, did their silence surprise you? So many Jews had assimilated. Surely they must have had working and personal relationships with their non-Jewish neighbors who would have protested this decree.
Esther: No, silence on the part of the non-Jewish world unfortunately didn't surprise me. The Jewish people have a long history of living in other countries, other than their own, of contributing greatly to the benefit of the host country, only to find themselves at a later time discriminated against, persecuted, and even cast out of the country for no logical reason.

Throughout time, we have lived in our homeland and been cast into exile from our homeland, only to find ourselves once again then rejected from the places we were forced initially to reside. This story has repeated itself so many times throughout history.

Why does that happen?

Esther: There are so many reasons for these mysterious phenomena. It has to do with our worthiness to live in the land of Israel according to Divine Will, as well as the mission of the Jewish people to heal, uplift, and perfect the rest of the world and ourselves by living in the midst of different host countries. Because the Jewish people have been charged with an important task of revealing God wherever they find themselves, they have been scattered all over the world. When the Jewish people do their job correctly, the nations are uplifted through them and receive much physical and spiritual blessing. Evil is diminished.

The Jewish people may not know this about themselves, but the enemy does. They are spiritually threatened by the goodness, the universality, and freedom within the message of the Jewish people. Leaders of these countries who seek to rule for their own nefarious reasons are threatened by the very existence of the Jewish people, so they are driven to destroy or oppress them. This is what happened in my time. The Jewish people were such a small minority in the Persian empire, they lived peacefully with their neighbors, and yet they alone were singled out for annihilation.

In the last generation the same thing happened. Under the leadership of Adolf Hitler and the Nazi party, Germany tried to annihilate the Jewish people who had lived within its country and in much of Europe for centuries. In this generation, we hear the threats and intentions of Iran, other Muslim nations, and terrorist groups to destroy the homeland of the Jewish people and annihilate the Jewish people once again.

Esther: This is an ancient battle. Nations that are particularly rooted in Edom, like Germany and much of Europe, or in Ishmael like Iran and many countries in the Arab world, at a certain point quite simply cannot tolerate the Godly light of the Jewish people. They are jealous, but it is even more than that. The very existence of the Jewish people is perceived as a direct challenge to the religions practiced in these countries as well as to the rulers who seek to dominate the world for their own selfish purposes.

The Jewish people serve as the conscience for the world and mirror back to evil dictators the ugliness of their deeds. Rather than change and become better people, the rulers in these nations scapegoat their moral, political, and economic failures onto the Jewish people. If the rulers can mobilize their people to hate the Jewish people, they will not be held accountable for the ways they have exploited and harmed their own. This tactic has been successful to direct their people's frustrations towards the Jewish people instead of their rulers who tyrannize them.

It does seem odd that the countries that seek the destruction of the Jewish people are terribly oppressive to their own. These rulers don't seem to care if their people suffer and even die in their effort to murder Jews. Their hatred of the Jewish people seems greater than their love for their own.

Esther: That is one of the biggest clues to identify a certain kind of primordial evil in the world. The Jewish people call this evil Amalek, named after the sworn enemy of the Jewish people in biblical time. Even though the Jewish people posed no threat to Amalek and the Jewish people were not even traveling near their territory, Amalek, a tribe of descendants of Esau, went out of its way to fight the Jewish people after their exodus from Egypt.

Is Amalek alive today? How can we identify Amalek?

Esther: Yes, Amalek is alive in your times once again. One of the ways to identify Amalek is that Amalek is an entity, either a person, group, or country that cannot tolerate the relationship that the Jewish people have with God. Amalek is also bent on destruction of the spiritual entity and integrity of the Jewish people, even if its proponents receive no real benefit from Israel's destruction. Their hatred is not logical and cannot be placated with bribes such as land for peace.

This is important to remember when dealing with Amalek. There is no bribing Amalek. That is why the Jewish people read the Torah portion about Amalek every year so they will remember what they must do when confronting Amalek. The Torah tells us, "Wipe out the memory of Amalek from under heaven. Do not forget" (Deut. 25:19). The people who may be identified as Amalek are so thoroughly evil, they cannot be healed or transformed. In my time, Haman was Amalek and was even a direct descendent from the tribe of Amalek.

If we look at history, there have been so many countries that do not want the Jewish people to live in their midst nor do they want them to live in their homeland. What are the Jewish people supposed to do?

Esther: You must understand that the enemies of the Jewish state of Israel are not just against the Jewish people, they are against God and all that is good. Remember, this is a most ancient battle. True God-believers love all of creation, especially the Jewish people. People who truly believe in God are not jealous of the faith of another, because they know deeply that God is one. Many non-believers in God are simply jealous of the special relationship that the Jewish people have with God and the gift of the land of Israel to the Jewish people. It is really quite simple.

I am worried by the rise of anti-Semitism in the world.

Esther: Do not worry; all will be good. In time, evil will be exposed for what it truly is and its power to mesmerize and seduce people will be diminished. The prophecies about the Jewish people, the rebuilding of the Holy Temple, and the messianic time, all will be fulfilled. That is the truth, no matter what the enemies of the Jewish people may say.

Israel is such a small country, yet it has made remarkable and even miraculous achievements that have benefited the entire world within the short time of its existence. It does not seem to matter what good Israel does. Israel, the one democracy in the region, that offers health, education, and voting rights to the Muslims who live in her midst, is considered a terrible occupier and oppressor by much of the world. Israel has received more proclamations against her in the United Nations than any other country. The surrounding Muslim nations treat their own citizens so poorly and women even worse, and some countries may even murder their own people and the United Nations does not censure them.

Esther: Israel is indeed the most beautiful and God-centered country in the world. No one should believe all the lies that are said about her. In time, it will be very clear for all to see that Israel, such a miniature country, is blessed and is a source of blessing for the entire world.

Though many want to occupy this country and claim it as their own, they do not yet realize that Israel only blossoms when the Jewish people live in it. Look what she has accomplished in such a short time, under so many challenging conditions. If another people would live in this holy land, they would not be prosperous.

There are many leaders and politicians from several countries, even the United States, who think that peace will come to the region if Jerusalem is divided between the Muslims and the Jews. What do you see from your heavenly station?

Esther: Dividing Jerusalem will not bring peace, only more war. Those who want to divide Jerusalem do not seek peace. They only seek to weaken Israel so as to destroy her. They fear the power of a unified Jerusalem upon the world. Jerusalem, the heart of the world, is that place in the future where God will rebuild the Holy Temple on the Temple Mount and fulfill and reveal the Divine purpose for all of creation. It is for that reason that the world does not want the Jewish people to rebuild the Holy Temple in Jerusalem.

Because of their intrinsic selfishness and jealousy, the nations of the world, even Jews who are disconnected from Judaism, do not see the importance of the rebuilding of the Holy Temple in Jerusalem. Jerusalem and the Holy Temple are a source of blessing for the entire world, not just the Jewish people. I instilled this within my son, so when he became king, he worked hard to liberate Jerusalem and rebuild the Holy Temple. It was his first accomplishment as he began his reign as king.

I pray that the readers and you, Queen Esther, will not mind indulging me a little more. I have such deep concern and am confused about what is happening today. Please forgive me for being so political. For so many years, the United States has tried diligently to be fair in brokering a peaceful settlement between Israel and the Arab peoples who seek to destroy her. Besides placing so much pressure upon Israel to give up land, the United States also gives the PLO and surrounding Muslim countries billions of dollars, trains their armies, and even sells advanced weaponry to sworn enemies of the Jewish people. It would appear that the United States thinks that with enough bribery there will be peace. What do you think?

Esther: If the United States of America does not align itself with Israel, and willingly even abandons the security of Israel in efforts to be fair, America will lose the blessings that have been bestowed upon it. This is most unfortunate. America in the hearts of its founding fathers was envisioned as a new Israel with a covenantal relationship with God modeled after that of the Jewish people. Because of this spiritual foundation, America became a very prosperous nation and a source of blessing to all. However, as the United States becomes increasingly secular, and is no longer governed by the highest moral values, it will no longer feel its primary affinity with Israel.

What about the fate of Israel if the United States does not support her? In addition to Iran, the surrounding Muslim countries have secured advanced missiles that can target any point in the land of Israel. As I speak to you now, the former official leadership in many of these countries is being overthrown and replaced with leaders who are Islamic fundamentalists who are more anti-Israel than the previous ones.

Esther: Do not worry that God's beloved country, the holy land of Israel, has very few friends, if any at all, among the nations of the world. This was true in my time and it will be true until the End of Days. Do not be dismayed. Israel does have the Holy One, the Creator of the universe, on her side, if and when the Jewish people honor their covenant with the Holy One, and that is more than enough. This is an ancient love affair that will soon be consummated. God is faithful. The people of Israel must not look to other nations for help, but realize that they have all that they need to be victorious. When they are aligned with Divine Will, they are protected.

Do you have a particular message for people today?

Esther: You live in extraordinary times. There is a great battle between good and evil underway once again in the world. When I lived, Persia was a great empire occupying one hundred twenty-seven provinces. In your time, Persia, now called Iran, is quickly spreading its tentacles to once again dominate the world for its own nefarious purposes. Battle lines are being drawn. This last battle will not be easy, but there is much blessing for those who are called to fight.

"Not by power, not by might, but by the spirit of the Lord," says the prophet Zechariah (Zech. 3:6). This last battle is primarily a spiritual war. Unlike previous wars, there are ultimately no political or military solutions for the conflicts in the world in your time. The stage is being set for an awesome Divine revelation. So rejoice.

What should people do today?

Esther: Even though the world may seem hopeless at times, and the challenges people face are so very great, the first and most important thing is to have faith and believe in the goodness of God. Trust that God will help you and fight this battle through you.

Nevertheless, you still must do your part. Everyone's contribution is needed because this battle is to be fought on many fronts. External enemies seeking to dominate and destroy others must be defeated externally. Internal enemies within each person such as doubt, hate, greed, and fear must also be overcome. Most people will not be called to battle the enemy physically, but still each must fight the battle against the evil inclination within themselves, families, and community.

Many people are not alarmed about what is happening in the world. They just want to have a good time.

Esther: What perhaps is most dangerous in your time is that many people prefer to live in the illusionary comfort of denial and fantasy. They have not yet recognized that there is a current battle for the soul of the world. Closing one's eyes does not make the danger disappear.

What was so miraculous in my time was that the Jewish people who were so divided among ourselves became unified because we woke up to see clearly that we shared the same fate as Jews. I pray that unity comes easily for Jews and all people who seek goodness in your time. Unfortunately, there may have to be additional wake-up calls in your time to remove the blinders of delusion to help people see clearly what is really taking place. In the interim do what you can to strengthen spiritual community and offer shelter to others.

What should we do?
Esther: There is power in community. I encourage everyone to join and support the Jewish people in continuing the holy work of eradicating evil externally and internally. Be part of a community dedicated to love and goodness whatever that may be. There is great power in unity. That is something that must be learned from the Purim story. When the Jewish people and good people all over the world are unified, they can accomplish much.

Everyone has all the resources needed to do what each can do to defeat evil. I needed to learn that, and so do many of you. If the situation worsens, organize fasts with prayer for the people. Fasting arouses greater Divine compassion and averts an evil decree. That is what I did and it worked. You can and must all be soldiers now. This battle must be fought on many fronts, internally and externally. Your prayers make a difference. Faith is your protection. Joy and love are your spiritual weapons. You are not powerless.

Do you have any particular guidance for the Jewish people?
Esther: The protection and strength of the Jewish people comes from their unity with each other and commitment to their covenant with God. The Jewish people become more vulnerable to evil when they are divided among themselves. When the Jews are united together in love and service, their enemies, who are truly God's enemies, will be destroyed. Miracles and blessing will be commonplace for them.

In my time, as I said earlier, the Jews were divided as they are in your time. There were primarily two groups: Jews who attended the orgies of the king, who ate non-kosher food, who assimilated with the general culture and were even willing to desecrate the vessels from the Holy Temple that were used at official parties; and Jews who refused to attend these affairs, and kept to themselves, occupying themselves with living a life devoted to Torah. These groups were very separate from each other and did not respect the choices of the other.

Haman saw these divisions clearly and tried to exploit them. The enemy of the Jewish people will always exploit the disunity within the Jewish community. When the Jews are divided, they are surely weakened and vulnerable as a people. This is true in all times.

Ultimately, as I said earlier, the Jewish people in my time were victorious because we overcame our differences and understood that we all shared the same fate as Jews. It was clear to everyone that there was no point in further ingratiating ourselves with our enemies. That kind of clarity will happen in your time. God willing, it will be sooner rather than later.

How do we create unity? There seems to be much divisiveness among people today.

Esther: Giving creates bonding. It is important for Jews as well as for all people in the world to give to others, for no other reason than to express love and unity with them. Every person must overcome the selfish desire to receive for oneself alone by sharing with others. Only by sharing and giving to others can one draw blessings into the world.

As a general rule, if you want to be connected to people, give to them. Life is all about sharing and giving. The quality of a person's life is enhanced greatly by acts of giving to others. When we give to others, not for what we will receive, but simply for the sake of giving, we become close to God, we internalize God, and we are filled with the Divine Spirit. It is for this reason that I instructed people to give gifts of food to each other and invite poor people to their homes for a Purim celebratory meal.

Do you have some final words to people?

Esther: Though you may never be in the kind of extraordinary situation like I was, everyone has opportunities in small and large ways to reveal God in their own way. Like me, you never know when you will be called upon to do something absolutely amazing. You can never fully appreciate the effect of all the good that you do. Let my story inspire and empower you with the courage and the faith to do what is difficult if it is the right thing to do, even what seems impossible, if it is necessary.

I send my love and blessings to you. May you take time to receive all the blessings generously bestowed upon you each day. May you be a blessing to others.

RESPONDING TO QUEEN ESTHER
(It is suggested that this be read out loud by the reader or group.)

> *Queen Esther, thank you for your inspiring words. You model to us the beauty, the heart and the power of the feminine. We can never thank you enough for the role you played in your lifetime to save the Jewish people. We honor you for your willingness to sacrifice your personal happiness for this cause as well as your courage to do what was difficult for you. Thank you for reminding us to make small and large gestures to create unity between people. We will do our share to create and strengthen community. May we also be empowered to validate and uplift others around us, like you did, with our love and innate joy.*

PRAYER TO THE GOD OF QUEEN ESTHER

> *May the God of Queen Esther empower me with the courage, faith, and creative intelligence to do what is difficult if asked and to know that all the resources needed to respond to any challenge before me are already within me. May I align myself with Divine Will and go forward in my life with trust and faith.*

What Quality of the Feminine Does Esther Demonstrate?

Esther, like Sarah, was considered to be one of the most beautiful women in the world, ever. This natural beauty radiated from her because of her alignment with the Divine Presence. Besides being beautiful inside and out, she used her beauty for holy purposes.

Esther modeled this power of the feminine in the most elevated way. In her preparation to see King Asherverous, she fasted and prayed rather than take that time to beautify herself physically with skin or makeup preparations. Even though she clearly understood that it was her sexual appeal as a woman that gave her a measure of power over the king, she knew that her power as a woman depended more on how she embodied the Divine Presence.

Like Esther, any woman aligned with God, regardless of her physical appearance, has a natural beautiful radiance that will make her attractive and appealing to men—and therefore have power over many men. The question before all women is whether they will use their inherent gifts and blessings of being feminine for noble holy purposes like Esther or primarily for their own benefit or gratification.

Another quality of the feminine that made Esther particularly beautiful was that she mirrored the beauty within others back to them. Everyone felt validated and elevated by Esther. To connect more with how Esther embodied the Divine Feminine, and to be more of an embodiment of the Divine Feminine yourself, make particular efforts each day to acknowledge the beauty within others.

How many people can you acknowledge and validate today or this week? Make a special effort to validate people in your immediate family. Sometimes these are the people we take for granted. Refrain from criticism of yourself and others. Loving and accepting yourself is the foundation for all the good you radiate to others.

What Meditative Practice Do We Learn from Esther?

The name Esther means "hidden." What is hidden is the domain of the feminine.

In seeking to attune to Esther or the feminine, we need to meditate and pray each day to find that place within us that is hidden, that is private, that is holy. Let go of what is external and come into the sacredness of life that lies deep within oneself. In this space of holy intimacy, there is only you and God. Surrender your ego self, your small self, and allow yourself to be permeated with the light of Shechinah until you identify with Her. From this place, you can draw down the strength to bring forth miracles in your life.

Remember that wherever you are, God is. Know that you are in the place that you are intended to be. God is with you. Nothing is by accident.

What Spiritual Practice Do We Learn from Esther?
The Spiritual Practice of Giving Gifts

In the celebration of the holiday of Purim that commemorates the miracles of Esther's time, there is a custom of giving gifts to friends that is called *mishloach manot,* or shortened to *shalach manot*. These gifts are simple offerings of fruit, nuts, wine, and cake that are distributed widely to friends, acquaintances, and even strangers. It can be just two items. Usually, these gifts are delivered through a third party, so their face is hidden and it feels that God is giving to the person.

Additionally, giving to the poor is encouraged at all times, but especially on Purim. "It is preferable to increase gifts to the poor rather than increasing *mishloach manot*" (Shulchan Aruch on the laws of *mishloach manot*).

Each day you are given opportunities to give to people in small or large ways. When we give to others in any way for any reason or for no reason at all, we are uplifted. Giving to others helps us to feel close to people.

Fast for Esther

In honor of Esther, make a spiritual connection with her on her fast day, the day preceding the holiday of Purim. Look at the Jewish calendar for what day it will be. Make efforts to fast, at least part of the day, and spiritually connect with the Jewish people. Dedicate your fast and prayer toward your own purification and the elimination of evil in the world. Join with Jews all over the world who pray that the consciousness of the wicked be turned to the Divine.

KEY QUESTIONS AND FOLLOW-UP DISCUSSION ON ESTHER

1. How does Esther's story inspire you to make your life better? What ways can you make this world better and defeat evil, even if it is just in your immediate circle?
2. How can you emulate Queen Esther? Can you emulate her speech pattern? Esther means hidden. Find the Esther within yourself. What is the hidden part within you that is the Esther within you?
3. How does this story of Esther help you to understand the role you can play to fight evil and selfishness and reveal more light and love in your personal life and in the world at large?
4. Many Jewish women view Vashti as a feminist because she refused to disrobe before the king. Young girls today are even dressing up as Vashti for Purim, even more than Queen Esther in some communities. Considering all the midrashim, teachings in the oral Torah, regarding her cruelty, do you feel that Vashti should be regarded as a model for young girls today? How do you understand this recent phenomenon?

CHAPTER TEN

MEDITATIONS AND CONTEMPLATIONS ON THE DIVINE PRESENCE

1.

Before there was time, before there was space, there was only Ain Sof, Limitless Light. That was all there was, only Ain Sof. There was nothing to bestow goodness upon, no one to be known by. The light of Ain Sof contracted and withdrew to create a void that would allow worlds to emerge as receptacles for the light of Ain Sof.

A line known as the kav, a rod of light, was extended into the void to sustain creation within Ain Sof. Not too much light to overwhelm creation, but enough to sustain it as the light became increasingly differentiated. The vessels that contained the light are also of the light. Everything is of the light, even the forces that oppose the light. Though Divine light is most concealed in our physical world, it was our physical world where the Divine intention is most realized. If the light of God is revealed too much, there would be no choice but to love God.

The goodness, the love, and the light of God are so overwhelming that we would be totally defenseless to choose otherwise. Only in this world of concealment is choice possible. Love requires freedom with the free will to choose love. Because of God's concealment, we feel a separate existence. Otherwise, there would be no one to love God in return.

God wants our love too. We are told to love God. Hear the words within you, "Love me with all your heart, soul, and might." Hear the Divine call for love resounding within you and rebounding back to God. God lives in your open loving heart. There is only one call to love. God's call to love is at the root of all other expressions of love.

2.

Imagine you can travel back in time before there was time and space. Visualize a hundred years, ten thousand years, one hundred thousand years. Travel back through time, until you realize that you can conceive of it no further. You touch a place that is called Infinity. Beyond Infinity is Ain Sof.

With your imagination, travel forward in time, ten years from now, a hundred years, ten thousand years, until you once again touch a place called Infinity. Beyond Infinity is Ain Sof, Limitless Light.

In your imagination, travel eastward, journey past China, leaving the orbit of our earth into the galaxy until you recognize that your imagination can take you no further and you again touch a place that we will call Infinity. Beyond Infinity is Ain Sof. Now travel westward, going past California, Hawaii, and out again into space, continuing as far as you can visualize, until you arrive once again at Infinity. Beyond Infinity, there is Ain Sof.

Repeat this meditation in all directions. Travel north and south, up and down similarly in your consciousness. Arrive in consciousness at a place that you recognize as Infinity. Know that even beyond infinity is Ain Sof.

Ain Sof surrounds Infinity. Then, sit, stand, and live in the expanded perception of Ain Sof, yet be simultaneously fully aware of the individualized expression of life that you know as you. You are alive in the middle of what you have identified as Infinity of Time and Space. Every point, every person, is the center point, the midpoint in Infinity.

Repeat silently to yourself, "I am the center point in Ain Sof. I am in the center of God." Internalize this awareness. Breathe and expand or contract your consciousness as much as you like, to the highest heights, to the deepest depths, to the greatest joy, to the most painful despair, yet you still remain within Ain Sof. There is truly nowhere else to be. Ain Sof encompasses all that was, is, and will be, in all places simultaneously.

Just as you were born out of your mother's womb, imagine that you are in God's womb. This is the truth. You are in the womb of the Divine Mother. This awareness is called the Makom, "the Place of the World." You feel yourself unconditionally loved and embraced when you live in the awareness of Makom.

"Bridle your mouth from speaking, and your heart from thinking, return to the Place," instructions from Sefer Yetzirah, the ancient manual for Kabbalistic meditation.

"Be Still and Know that I am God" (Ps. 46:10). Silence is the highest praise of God.

3.

Your soul, created out of the light of Ain Sof, descended into this physical world to reveal a greater light, for light shines brightest amidst the darkness. It was a dangerous mission because it required that you forget what was previously known and discover it once again anew.

For the limited time you occupy a physical body, you have been charged to bring the light of the upper worlds to the lower worlds, to make unifications between the physical and spiritual. Godliness is revealed through these unifications. Your spiritual wings have been clipped while you occupy a physical body so you remain grounded enough to fulfill your mission. However, you can still ascend to the upper worlds when you take time to quiet the mind, open the heart, and attune to your soul frequency.

Listen, deep inside, to the inner voice within your own heart and soul. Listen to your thirst for the light and even of your yearning to return home to the place of luminous light revealed. In these moments, you are reminded of your mission, and guided to fulfill your purpose. Reveal Godliness in your midst. Be God's candle and shine the light for all to see. What one can do in the physical world is very great. Do not delay. The world is depending on you.

4.

Because you now live in a physical body, you may lose perspective from time to time, and entertain illusions that you are separate, independent, and limited. You are not. You may feel separate, but as the Divine soul, your true essence, you are not. You may feel yourself an independent entity, but you, as the Divine soul, are a part of God. You are interconnected with all of Creation. You may feel limited by time and space, but you are not. Your reality is not confined to the physical world, nor limited by the five senses with which you have been gifted.

Even though you live in a designated space known as a physical body, you need not be limited or defined by it. You may live in a material world, but you are not of it. You are so much more. You are an expression of Ain Sof. You have even been told that you are created in the likeness and image of the Divine.

Repeat, "I am created in the image and likeness of the Divine." Internalize this message by repeating it many times and meditating upon it often. You are not separate from the Light that creates, permeates, sustains, and surrounds you. You are in essence a ray of the light of Ain Sof.

Meditate to enter the doorway into the consciousness of God, who lives within you, at your core, in your heart of hearts, as you. See through the garments God wears in the world. Everything that happens is a Divine message. When you truly welcome God into your life and invite God to reside within you, God is the most holy loving treasured guest who will never leave you. God is faithful. God is with you at all times, in the good and in the bad, even when you are unaware of God. From time to time, know that it is God who orchestrates events in your life.

So call out to God and receive all the love and wisdom that God has hidden away for you. It was for this love and knowledge you were created. Words are inadequate to express our appreciation for all that is bestowed upon us each day.

CHAPTER ELEVEN

BIBLICAL PROPHECIES AND AMERICA'S FATE

Biblical prophecies provide an invaluable guide toward understanding current and future world events. They offer believers profound consolation and faith that the yet unfulfilled prophecies will be fulfilled in due time. From a Jewish perspective, world events are not random or accidental. The return of the Jewish people to their ancestral homeland after two thousand years of exile, the aggressiveness of Muslims, and the decline of Europe are just a few examples of prophecies being revealed today. We live in auspicious times! A question remains. What will be the fate of America? Will it be aligned with the fate of Israel or that of Europe?

In light of the upcoming 2016 presidential elections this year, I have added this additional chapter as my personal and desperate plea for America, for its own sake, to choose a president who unabashedly supports Israel. In making my case, I have even presented a historical perspective to further argue that there is no moral equivalence between Israel and her enemies. America faces an important and clear choice. The election of the next president in 2016 may possibly seal America's fate.

The Bible tells us "Those who bless you [Israel and the Jewish people] will be blessed. Those who curse you will be cursed" (Gen. 27:29). If America is faithful to its own spiritual covenant with God, and supports Israel unequivocally, America will be blessed with prosperity and protection.

On one hand, America has a natural affinity towards Israel because the founding fathers envisioned America as a new Israel with a covenant modeled after that of the Jewish people. However, America has become increasingly secular and progressive. Consequently, many Americans today do not feel an affinity towards Israel. If America continues in this path, its fate will be vastly different.

The Bible is clear. The United States brings physical and spiritual harm upon itself when it acts in ways which do not support the Jewish State of Israel. For example, when America pressures Israel to make dangerous concessions to its enemies, it experiences an almost immediate natural disaster, such as a hurricane, flood, wild fire.

Rabbi Menachem Kohen's important book, *Prophecies for the Era of Muslim Terror*, documents numerous examples of natural and man-made disasters for America's failure to support Israel in the years between October 1991 and October 2004. The first World Trade Center bombing on February 26, 1993, occurred shortly after President Clinton sent his secretary of state to eight Arab Muslim countries to develop a strategy against Israel. On September 10, 2001, a new plan to force Jews out of parts of Israel and not defend itself from Arab attacks was completed; a day before the September 11 attacks.

In 2004, during the months of August and September, America experienced Hurricanes Charley, Frances, Ivan, and Jeanne. At that very time, America under President Bush demanded the cessation of new housing construction, pressured Israel to expel Jews from Gaza, and even addressed the United Nations to impose a settlement freeze in Israel.

The prophet Joel reminds us, "I will execute judgment upon them for what they did to my people, by partitioning My land" (Joel 4:2). The Talmud, the rabbinical commentary on the Bible, informs us that, "When the people of Israel suffer, when their lives are in jeopardy, the Almighty marshals the forces of nature and unleashes them and there are rumbling disturbances i.e. earthquakes, tornadoes, et cetera." (Babylonian Talmud).

The world also suffers when America does not fully support Israel. America's efforts to be a fair broker in negotiating a two state solution between Israel and the PLO, a terrorist entity whose charter calls for the destruction of the State of Israel, has not led to peace but rather increased terrorism in Israel and throughout the world. In so many instances, the United States pressured Israel to make dangerous concessions in the name of peace but did not place similar pressure on the Arabs to even refrain from acts of terrorism. Whether it is a Democratic or Republican presidency, it appears that America keeps doing the same thing and expects a different result. All America's efforts for peace fail because they never address the real fundamental reason for the lack of peace. It is not Israeli settlements or anything Israel does. Rather, it is the PLO's resistance to the very existence of a Jewish State. Why America chooses to not attach financial consequences for the PLO's support of terrorism is a mystery. This lack of moral clarity in the Middle East on the part of America has made the world more dangerous by signaling to Islamic terrorists they can act with virtual impunity.

Like a dormant cancer in the world body, the brutality of Islam had been largely contained for thousands of years—until recently. The abandonment of an

American leadership role on the world stage (particularly under President Obama's administration) released the brutality of Islam more horribly upon the world than ever before. ISIS would not have existed as the terrorizing force that it is in the world had the United States contained it early on. Unfortunately, President Obama chose not to listen to his military advisors and vacated American troops from Iraq. Until the atrocities of ISIS became so horrifying, President Obama dismissed it as a JV team and did little to contain it early on when it would have been easy to do so. Now ISIS murders people mercilessly all over the world.

As a direct result of the failure of America's international policies in the Middle East, the world is now being set up for one of the greatest battles between good and evil of all time, as predicted in biblical Scripture. The Divine Plan warrants that this battle be waged in every generation, until the evil in every person and in every nation is finally defeated. Since the beginning of time, this battle has been waged between good and evil, spirituality and materialism. With daily acts of violence and terrorism taking place somewhere in the world, this battle is heating up in intensity. Many people even believe that we may be living in the prophesied End Times.

The proponents of Radical Islam have clearly stated and acted upon their intention to establish a global Islamic caliphate, impose Sharia law, and convert or murder all non-Muslims in the world by any means. They have declared war on the world. ISIS, Iran, Hezbollah, PLO, Hamas, and numerous other Islamic terrorist entities all have the same vision and purpose. Nothing is too ruthless or brutal for them. Beheadings of children and adults, burning people alive, hanging teenagers for listening to Western music, raping little girls, kicking newborn babies to their deaths, and so much more, are recent examples of their brutality.

This may be the worst face of evil the world has ever seen. Unlike the evil perpetrators in the past such as Nazis or Stalinists, these Islamic jihadists make no effort to hide these atrocities. They even post them in videos on social media to inspire more terror and recruit others. These jihadists also do not fear death, unlike our previous foes. Rather, they rejoice and embrace death when it is as an opportunity to kill others. The potential for the use of nuclear and biological warfare on their part only intensifies the stakes today.

In the prophecy given to Hagar regarding her descendants, the Bible predicted, "He shall be a wild ass of a man. His hand shall be against everyone" (Gen. 16:12). Hagar is the acknowledged mother of the people of Ishmael, the father of Muslims. We are seeing today the fulfillment of this prophecy.

The majority of wars and violence in today's world is done in the name of Islam. The Zohar tells us, "Muslims will wage violent wars throughout the world in the pre-messianic era" (Zohar II, 32A). Of course, not all Muslims are radical jihadists, but there are countless committed zealots and many more sympathizers. With over a billion and a half Muslims on the planet today, even a small percentage of this number would indicate millions of potential jihadists and sympathizers.

Unfortunately, the success of Islamic terrorism appears to be radicalizing additional Muslims at a greater speed than ever before. Both ISIS and Iran have communicated plans to capture and dominate Islamic countries in the Middle East, the entirety of Europe and the United States. The frightening possibility exists now that ISIS and Iran will swallow up the other Muslim nations and terrorist entities.

This is not a new battle. Islam's hatred of Jews and Christians is ancient. Passages within the Koran even require such hatred.

"The Prophet said . . . the last hour would not come unless the Muslims will fight the Jews and the Muslims will kill them until the Jews would hide themselves behind a stone or a tree and a stone or tree would say: Muslim or the servant of Allah, there is a Jew behind me, come and kill him" (Sahib Muslim book 041# 6985).

This frequently quoted verse from Muslim scriptures is only one example of many. Muslims are also commanded to kill other Muslims who refuse to accept Sharia law or if they convert to Christianity. In recent years, radical Muslims have murdered over a quarter of a million people, Muslims and Christians in Syria. No longer confined to a particular physical space, radical jihadists are now committing brutal acts of terrorism all over the world.

This ruthless behavior of Radical Islam today dates back to Mohammed who founded Islam. Mohammed himself ordered the beheading and the slaughtering of thousands of Jews who were unwilling to accept him as their prophet. He instructed his followers to emulate him for all time. From Spain to Iraq to Afghanistan and Yemen, Jews living under Muslim rule were forced to convert, pay a tax, or be killed.

Prior to 1948, Jews in Israel (known as Palestine at the time) suffered from numerous pogroms and massacres by Muslims. At the encouragement of the Grand Mufti of Jerusalem, acknowledged as the grandfather of the PLO, thousands of Muslims even traveled to Germany during World War II to fight with Hitler. The Grand Mufti himself went to Germany to encourage Hitler to systematically murder the Jewish people. The Grand Mufti announced in a March 1st, Arabic broadcast from Berlin, "Kill the Jews wherever you find them. It would please God, history and religion." Not commonly known, the Palestinian movement for statehood is an outgrowth of Nazism. On January 9th, 2013, Mohammed Abbas, the leader of the PLO, a Holocaust denier, honored the

Nazi collaborator. "We must remember and honor the Grand Mufti of Palestine." Even in 2016, Hitler's *Mein Kampf* and the anti-Semitic *Protocols of the Elders of Zion* continue to feature prominently in the PLO education system. In spite of the billions of dollars the PLO has received from nations of the world, its charter and mission statement clearly state its primary commitment to the destruction of the Jewish State of Israel. They have suffered no consequences for refusing to change their charter or their education system.

The twenty-two Muslim nations surrounding Israel have been officially and unofficially at war with the miniature Jewish State of Israel since its inception in 1948. Rabbi Kohen provides an interesting picture of Israel. Israel has approximately six million Jews who are surrounded by four hundred million Arabs. The entire country of Israel has a population equal to that of Madrid. The land of Israel now totals seven thousand square miles, while the adjacent Muslim territory is more than six million, seven hundred thousand square miles. Rabbi Kohen likens Israel to a tiny playing card in a huge football field inhabited by Muslims.

Despite its size, Israel has offered the entire world, including those living in Muslim countries, advanced technological, medical, agricultural, and irrigation innovations. Technology like the cell phone was created in Israel, yet the very presence of Jews in their midst is more than many Muslims can stomach, even though they benefit and use everything that Israel has created.

Just one day after the United Nation's ratification of the State of Israel, five surrounding Arab nations attacked. "Drive the Jewish people into the Sea" was and remains their frequent battle cry. Almost simultaneously, the surrounding Muslim nations, Syria, Iraq, and Lebanon heartlessly expelled approximately eight hundred thousand Jews from their borders. These Jews had lived peacefully in these countries for thousands of years. Exiled, they had to leave most of their worldly wealth and possessions behind. Egypt similarly expelled its Jews a little later in the early 1950s.

Most of these Jews from Arab countries immigrated to Israel. As Israel fought this war of independence with the surrounding Muslim countries, it also had the challenging task of integrating a new emigrating population. In addition to those expelled from Arab countries, there were many Holocaust survivors languishing in Displaced Person camps who were smuggled into Israel.

The establishment of the Jewish state of Israel in 1948 after two thousand years of exile is one of the most important fulfillments of a biblical prophecy in our time. This is particularly significant for Jews and Christians because other prophecies regarding the messiah cannot take place until the Jewish State was established. The Jewish State of Israel is a real deal changer for the world.

Unfortunately, it took the ashes of six million Jews to finally open the hearts of the nations of the world to allow the Jewish people to re-establish a Jewish State.

Though the United Nations officially allocated the land of Israel for the Jewish people in 1948, believers see the Bible as the Jewish people's deed to the land of Israel. The Jewish people were gifted with the land of Israel numerous times throughout the Bible. The exile and the return of the Jewish people to their ancestral homeland has been described in great detail by numerous later prophets. Here are a few examples:

"Behold the days are coming, says the Almighty . . . I will bring back the captives of My people Israel. They will rebuild desolate cities and settle them. They will plant vineyards and drink their wine, they will cultivate gardens and eat their fruits. I will plant them on the land and they will never again be uprooted from their land that I have given them" (Amos 9:14–15).

"But you, the mountain of Israel, you will give forth blossoming branches and produce luscious fruit for My people Israel, for they are soon to arrive. They will inherit the land which will be theirs for a possession and the Land will never again be bereaved of them" Ezekiel 36: 8–12).

Even the Koran declares that Israel belongs to the Jewish people. "Bear in mind the words of Moses to his people. . . . Enter, my people, the Holy land which Allah has assigned for you" (Surah 5:20–21).

The land of Israel is integral to the identity of the Jewish people. Since the destruction of its Holy Temple in Jerusalem thousands of years ago, Jews all over the world have prayed three times a day to return to their ancestral holy land and rebuild the Holy Temple to be a source of light and blessing to the entire world. People may not know that hundreds and thousands of Jews will not even eat a piece of bread without uttering such prayers. At every Jewish wedding for two thousand years, a glass in broken to remind us that our joy as Jews is diminished because we have not yet built the Holy Temple on the Temple Mount.

The land of Israel and the establishment of the Holy Temple has always been envisioned as an essential base of operation needed for the Jewish people to fulfill their spiritual mission of uplifting the world. Because of the holiness and potency of this mission, the ownership of Israel has been brutally contested by those who seek to dominate the world for their own nefarious purposes throughout history, even up to today. The Jewish people settled in the land of Israel and built it into a world power in ancient times. Ultimately on two occasions, the Jewish Holy Temple in Jerusalem was destroyed and the majority of Jews were either murdered or expelled from the land of Israel. To escape persecution and death, some of these expelled Jews converted to Islam and Christianity depending on the dominant religion of the country that now hosted them.

In the oral tradition within Judaism, Rachel asks God, "Why are you jealous of idolatry, which has no substance? Why did you exile my children and let the enemies slaughter them?" At once, the compassion of the Holy One, Blessed be He, was aroused and He said, "For Rachel, I will return the people of Israel to their place" (Pesika Eichah Rabbasi 24). This prophecy is taking place before us. Jews are returning to their ancestral homeland from all over the world.

The land of Israel was largely uninhabited for two thousand years, ever since the destruction of the second Holy Temple. The United Nations would not have allocated the establishment of a Jewish homeland in a land hosting a large indigenous Muslim population.

God tells us in the Bible, "I will make your cities a waste. I will bring the land into desolation. Then I will remember My covenant with Jacob, and I will remember the Land" (. Lev. 26:32). There was a drought in the land of Israel for more than one thousand eight hundred years. When the State of Israel was established, the rain miraculously resumed. "The cities in the Land of Israel will be inhabited, the ruins will be rebuilt ... I will make it better than it ever was" (Ezek. 36:10–11). Israel is now such a vibrant and beautiful country. Due to Divine blessing, the Jewish people have transformed the desert into gardens and farms. They have even exported their innovative agricultural techniques to help many other countries.

It is important to remember that the United Nations originally offered a two state solution for the Jewish people and Muslims in 1948. There was to be a Jewish homeland in the land of Israel and an Arab homeland in Jordan. This United Nations resolution was never accepted by its surrounding Muslim nations.

The 1948 War of Independence began the day after the UN ratification of the State of Israel, and the Jewish people lost a part of Jerusalem and the West Bank that had been previously allocated to them. The land was mostly reclaimed by Israel in the Six Day War of 1967. It was Jordan that occupied Jewish land but no one cared about that. After a humiliating Arab defeat in the War of 1967, Arabs began a propaganda campaign to oppose the occupation and attempt to establish another Muslim state in Jerusalem and also on the land that was originally allocated to the Jewish people.

Initially, the Jewish people conceded to the Arab request for another State because they were willing to share the holy land with Muslims in the hope that would finally bring peace. The creation of another Palestinian state was also pressured by the United States. With continuous brutal acts of terrorism perpetuated by the PLO, these fantasies of peace on the part of most Israelis and many others have been largely destroyed. Nevertheless, Europe and America continue to press for a Palestinian state that would be oppressive to Arabs and dangerous to the security of Israel.

One of the most troubling of prophecies from the prophet Zechariah relating to Ishmael is the following: "The children of Ishmael will rouse all the peoples of the world to come up to war against Jerusalem, as it is written I will gather all the nations of the world against Jerusalem to battle" (Zohar II:8b, and Zech. 14:2).

This prophecy is also being fulfilled before our eyes today. As predicted, Muslim nations at the UN repeatedly attempt to discredit and penalize Israel with many untrue accusations. The democratic country of Israel with the highest human rights standards in the Middle East receives the majority of censures by the United Nations. Arabs, blessed to live in the land of Israel, enjoy full citizenship with extraordinary health and education opportunities unparalleled in the Muslim world. Muslim countries that oppress and even murder their own citizens receive no censure at all. Until recently, the United States had stood, sometimes alone, as an ally of Israel. The Obama administration's continued alignment with Israel at the United Nations is now in question.

The Zohar predicts that Ishmael will rise to dominate the world and the secular Christian world will decline. We do not have to be prophets to see what is taking place in Europe today. Not only is there a dramatic increase in crimes such as rape and violence committed by Muslims there, the character of Europe is changing. Europe is now being weakened by a large immigration of Muslims who are largely anti-Semitic.

The high birth rate of Muslims will lead to the people of Ishmael taking over Europe not by war but by demographics. The recent efforts in Europe to boycott Israeli products on the Israeli land known as the territories, may be an effort of appeasement towards its Muslim citizens and Arab nations. In spite of its tremendous budgetary constraints, Europe continues to support the PLO and Hamas with billions of dollars. Why? Is it because European anti-Semitism has once again risen to levels comparable to that of World War II when over six million Jews were brutally murdered? In a few years, there may be no Jews remaining in Europe as it is no longer safe for them to live there.

The decline of Christian nations is forecasted in Rebecca's prophecy. Rebecca, the mother of twin brothers Jacob and Esau, was told, "Two nations in your womb. Two regimes from your insides shall be separated. The might shall pass from one regime to the other. And the elder shall serve the younger" (Gen. 25:23).

THIS IS THE MOST IMPORTANT MESSAGE FOR OUR TIMES.

According to Jewish wisdom, Esau is code for Europe and the Christian and secular countries. Yakov is code for Israel and the Jewish people. When Esau is dominant, Yakov is weakened. As predicted in Rebecca's prophecy, this will change in the future. This change is taking place right now before our eyes. The Christian secular nations that lauded themselves over the Jewish people for thousands of years are now being weakened.

When I first understood the significance of this prophecy, I could not envision how Europe would be further weakened. Now everyone can see this all too clearly. God is using the Muslims to weaken Europe. We are also witnessing the rise of the Jewish State of Israel at the same time. The Jewish people who had been in a weakened state until they regained their homeland in 1948 are getting stronger with each day.

Biblical prophecy tells us that Israel will emerge as a world super power. "If any of the nations do not come up to Jerusalem . . . there will be no rain upon it" (Zech. 14:17). Already Israel gives security and technological guidance to many countries in the world. A recent example at the time of the writing of this chapter is that Israel had warned Brussels about the pending terrorist attack in March 2016. Brussels failed to listen. Now Belgium, along with many other countries, even the United States of America, is asking little Israel for help.

As predicted in Rebecca's prophecy, Esau will serve Yakov. As explained in the interview with Rebecca, this prophecy essentially means that Christian secular nations will ultimately accept the spiritual principles of faith, morality, and God that are at the core of Jewish spiritual mission.

Who is Esau, and how do we identify Esau? Esau in the biblical story sold his birthright of the first born for a pot of lentils because he was hungry. In this act, Esau demonstrated that satisfying his physical needs and desires was more important to him than the spiritual privileges and responsibilities of the firstborn. Esau was also said to be a murderer, an adulterer, and even an idolater, but he pretended to be righteous before his father. Materialism and hypocrisy are the primary characteristics of people associated with Esau.

The Bible tells us that "Esau hated Jacob" (Gen. 27:41). When we take into account this ancient hatred, we should not be surprised that Jews were expelled, discriminated against, persecuted, and even slaughtered intermittently in Europe and in Russia for thousands of years. During the Holocaust, Jews were even prevented from entering the United States or Israel. Consequently, most were condemned to a sure death in concentrations camps. European anti-Semitism continues even today.

Esau and Ishmael sometimes join together in their mutual hatred of the Jewish people. In many ways, the predominantly Christian nation of America has shown herself to be in the camp of Esau, aligned more with Europe and Islam than with Israel. For example, in a series of many betrayals, the greatest betrayal of Israel by the United States might be the recent Iran Deal aggressively pursued by President Obama. Against the desperate cries of Israel and most of American Jewry, this deal assured Iran becoming a nuclear power and receiving billions of dollars to pursue its evil agenda. In negotiating this deal, the US failed to demand that Iran give up its call for the destruction of the State of Israel and support of international terrorism. It did not even take a stand against the wanton murder of Iran's own citizens.

President Obama wanted this Iran deal at almost any cost. He ultimately caved in to most of Iran's demands. Within a month of the release of Iranian monies, Iran purchased advanced weaponry from Russia, which later transferred to their proxies like Hezbollah and Hamas. In very little time, they conducted ballistic missile tests which violated the deal. To date, there have been no American repercussions for these violations.

The Palestinian and Israeli conflict is another important example of the United States having lessened its commitment to the State of Israel. American leaders often talk about being a fair broker between a beautiful democratic country and a corrupt terrorist entity called the PLO that oppresses its own people, encourages acts of terrorism, and is sworn to the destruction of the State of Israel. It is well known that monies given to the PLO by the United States and Europe are used to purchase weaponry for war against Israel, reward people who commit terrorism against the Jewish people, and make billionaires of Muslim leadership.

The PLO annually spends millions of dollars in salaries just to imprisoned terrorists who have murdered Jews. According to Palestinian Media Watch, terrorists murdering large groups of people or children are paid much more than those who murder only one or two people. Monthly salaries range from $750 to $3,750. Upon exiting prison, terrorists receive an additional $35,000. Interestingly enough, these prisoner salaries are listed as part of the Palestinian Authority's general salary budget, which includes salaries of civil servants. That is most telling about how the PLO views terrorism. Terrorists are seen as employees of the PLO.

The PLO also erects monuments and dedicates city squares to honor its terrorists. In recent years, the United States pressured Israel to release Muslim terrorists with blood on their hands just to get the PLO to the negotiation table. Does the PLO resemble a country seeking peace? Where does all this money come from to pay the terrorists? This is your tax dollars at work.

Why does America support the PLO? Does America really believe the Arab false narrative of the terrible occupation by Israel? Can it not see that the only oppression of people who identify as Palestinians is from its own leadership, and not from Israel? Muslim and Christian Arab citizens of Israel have more civil rights and better health care and education than anywhere else in the Arab world. Does America want another corrupt, apartheid, tyrannical, oppressive Muslim country dedicated to the destruction of Israel?

Does America not even care about Arabs? It is a mystery why America would support the establishment of another tyrannical oppressive Muslim state to be called Palestine when there are already twenty two such Muslim countries already, and sixty countries with a Muslim majority in the world. I used to think it was because of oil. But America is now a producer of oil and natural gas. It must mean that America feels some affinity to these Muslims.

Despite the PLO's oppression of its own citizens, the United States continues its support for a Palestinian State. The United States even protests when Israel builds apartment buildings in Jerusalem and on land designated as the West Bank, known as Section C. This is land that has not been delineated as part of the proposed Palestinian State. This land was originally allocated to Israel at the time of its establishment, lost to Jordan in the War of Independence in 1948, but recaptured in 1967.

Under the presidency of Barak Hussein Obama, the United States even supports boycott of Israeli products. There is concern that the US will not veto the PLO's upcoming censure of Israel at the United Nations. Obama has threatened to not cast the single veto in the United Nations Security Council as America has in the past to protect Israel. This is very troubling but it would be a fulfillment of a biblical prophecy. All the nations of the world would be united against this miniature, beautiful, holy, democratic country called Israel.

If the United States continues in its present direction, it must definitely be considered a part of Esau. As such, America will consequently suffer the fate of Esau. Like Europe, America will be weakened. This weakening of America has already begun.

Many people are unaware of the Zohar's profundity. The Zohar predicted the day of the attack on September 11. "Three very tall towers will collapse on the 23rd day of Elul, and a fourth one will be struck, in a city, in a predominantly Christian country. The collapse of the buildings will be accompanied by a thunder-like sound and tremendous fire" (Zohar III, 212b). The fourth building was not described as being in the same locale as the first three. We did not know the year or the exact place, but September 11 corresponds to the Hebrew month of Elul, the 23rd day in the year 2001. The United States would then spiritually be considered a part of Esau.

There is another possible fate for the United States. It can attach itself to the Jewish people and receive the blessings reserved for it. It is natural for the United States to do this. The United States has always had a different spiritual mission and identity than that of Europe. America never engaged in anti-Semitism to the extent of Europe. For the most part, America has supported religious freedom for all people, a very Jewish principle.

There are two divisions within the Christian world. Replacement Theologians believe Christianity has replaced Judaism. According to Replacement Theology, Jews have suffered because they did not convert to Christianity. The fact that Jews continue to exist and that there is a Jewish State of Israel is threatening to those who hold by Replacement Theology. Dominant in Europe, it provided fertile ground for the Holocaust. The Catholic Church, largely anti-Semitic, watered the spiritual soil for the acceptance and proliferation of Nazism.

Dispensationalism is the other school within Christianity, more dominant in the United States than Europe. The Christian world in America largely rejected Replacement Theology. They mostly feel they owe the Jewish people a debt of gratitude for the essentials of their faith. They totally understand that if the United States supports Israel, America will be protected. These Christians visit Israel as much as Jews, and give financially to Israel as well. Many even embrace some Jewish rituals. The bonds between these Christians and Israel are strengthening each day.

The murder of more than one third of the world's Jewry in the Holocaust in Europe in the 1940s was the culmination of thousands of years of frequent pogroms, persecution, and discrimination. Because of this karma, the secular materialistic Christian world is now in decline as the power of Ishmael rises. This shift of power has been predicted. " The day of the Lord is near for all nations. As you have done to Israel, it will be done to you. Your deeds will return upon your own head" (Obad. 1:15). Jews are now fleeing Europe to Israel in increasing numbers for safety. Muslims are now terrorizing Europe in increasing and more frequent terrorist attacks. The reign of Ishmael in the world is forecasted to be a most dreadful time. Many Jewish sages even expressed their hope to not be alive during this time period known as the Messianic time.

There are many prophecies suggesting even a worldwide mass murder of millions of people. The prophet Zechariah declares, "There will be a day which will be the Lord's day, the day which the Holy One has appointed for taking vengeance on the idolatrous nations" (Zech. 14:2). Zechariah's prophecies are more descriptive regarding those who wage war against Jerusalem. "Their flesh will rot while they stand on their feet, their eyes will rot in their sockets and their tongues will rot in their mouths" (Zech. 14:12). "It will be a period of great troubles--the likes of which were never before experienced" (Dan. 12:1).

Sounds frightening like nuclear or biological warfare.

There are two minor players on the world stage included in Biblical prophecies but are not as well known. They are also important to identify so they can also be fought. The first one is called, "Erev Rav," the mixed multitudes. When Moses took the Jewish people out of Egypt, more than two thirds of the people who went out with Moses were Egyptian. These are the people who are called the Erev Rav. They are the people who built the Golden Calf. Throughout time, some of the souls of these people continue to reincarnate and cause havoc for the Jewish people. These may be the Jews who censure Israel and collaborate with the people who seek her destruction.

The Jewish Voice of Peace, J Street, and other left-wing Jewish organizations, seem to be dedicated to destroying the credibility and legitimacy of the Jewish state of Israel. They do not mind accepting Arab money to carry out this mission. When you see segments of the Jewish people actively working against the Jewish State of Israel, you now know who they are and how to identify them. Unfortunately, there are many Jews who are not part of the Erev Rav soul group but they do not yet recognize or accept their unique and covenantal relationship with God. They may be sympathetic to the Erev Rav because they are ignorant and greatly assimilated. These people can be educated and healed with the love of God and the Bible.

Much like in ancient times, even in the midst of open miracles, there were always Jews who doubted and rebelled. There has always been a tension within the Jewish people of those who want to be like all the other nations and those who want to fulfill the spiritual mission assigned to the Jewish people since the time of Abraham and Sarah. It is predicted that the Erev Rav will rise in power and later be defeated. In the 1700s, the esteemed and saintly teacher known as the Vilna Gaon in his book *The Voice of the Turtledove* identified the Erev Rav as the greatest future enemy of the Jewish people.

The final important player on the world stage is "Amalek." This refers to the ancient tribe who went out of their way to fight and destroy the Jewish people. When the Jewish people left Egypt they were not passing the lands inhabited by Amalek, but the Amalekites went out of their way to attack the Jewish people. There was no reason to attack them other than hatred.

People who are to be identified as Amalekite cannot bear that the Jewish people have a unique covenant with God. **The Bible instructed us to not negotiate with Amalek**. "Remember what Amalek did to you on your journey out of Egypt" (Deut. 25:17). Their hatred is not logical. They cannot be bribed, only defeated. Also in his book, *The Voice of the Turtledove*, the Vilna Gaon identified the war against Amalek in three ways.

1. Amalek of the heart—that is the evil inclination and vices within. This is the critical judgmental voice within the heart, of the person. Amalek is the voice of doubt. The Hebrew letters of Amalek and Safek (the Hebrew word for doubt) have the same numerical value. As individuals, we must do our inner spiritual healing work to restore faith as the center of our lives and weaken the hold of doubt and negativity within us.
2. The spirit of Amalek, referring to Satan, the adversary of Israel. His main power is in the gates of Jerusalem when its lands are desolate. The resettling and building up of the land of Israel is weakening this spirit of Amalek.
3. The material physical form of Amalek comprises a major part of Esau, Ishmael, and the mixed multitude. The Vilna Gaon told the Jews to wage this war against Amalek by planting themselves in the land of Israel and fulfilling the commandments that can only be fulfilled there. Rebuilding of the land of Israel with all the mitzvot (commandments) that can only be performed there will mitigate evil in the entire world.

Amalek emerges in almost every generation. Hitler was Amalek in the last generation. Radical Islam such as ISIS, the leadership of Iran, Hamas, and the PLO are clearly Amalek today. America's attempt to negotiate a deal with countries or entities that are part of Amalek is both foolish and dangerous. It is also against biblical instructions.

The Bible tells us, "Wipe out Amalek" (Deut. 25:19). These biblical verses remind us that ISIS cannot be contained, only defeated. You cannot negotiate with those who are sworn to the destruction of the Jewish State of Israel. To fight Amalek is to fight with God against evil. "God wages war against Amalek from generation to generation" (Exodus 17:16). As Queen Esther stated in her interview. "You must understand that the enemies of the Jewish State of Israel are not just against the Jewish people, they are against God and all that is good. Remember, this is a most ancient battle. People who truly believe in God are not jealous of the faith of another, because they know deeply that God is one. Many non-believers in God are simply jealous of the special relationship that the Jewish people have with God and the gift of the Land of Israel to the Jewish people. It is really quite simple."

The Talmud, written thousands of years ago, revealed that Iran (ancient Persia) will be the greatest threat in the future. That is why this current Iran Deal is so frightening and dangerous. It even guarantees that Iran will build a nuclear bomb after ten years, if not before. The Talmud told us there will be a day when the Jews will cry out in fear against Persia.

The Talmud records a message to the Jews of the future. "Why are you afraid now? The day of your redemption has arrived" (Gemara Sanhedrin 97:2). The chapter on Queen Esther, who defeated Amalek in ancient Persia, is so important, for she gave instructions on what is needed to defeat Iran in our time.

It is important to emphasize that frightening doomsday prophecies are not written in stone. **America's fate can be changed through prayer, returning to God, and doing good deeds**. It is for this reason that I am writing this book. There is a battle for the soul of America today. America was founded on Judaic/Christian principles. If America honors her foundation, she will thrive. Psalm 1 reminds us of the benefits of fulfilling biblical teachings. "He will be like a tree, set into the ground near streams of water, which yields fruits in its season, and whose leaf does not wither. In whatever he does, he will succeed" (Psalm 1:3). May this be America's fate! If America chooses to not be connected to her spiritual roots, or to God, the fruits of America will wither. America will be vibrant only when it chooses to support the spiritual principles within her own constitution and the Jewish state of Israel.

In conclusion, I, along with millions of people of all faiths, pray each day for inner and outer peace for all people. May the consciousness of every person be awakened to the love of God and God's creation, however they envision God to be. May America join Israel in transforming the world to a place of peace, love, and joy. God bless America and her people.

CONCLUSION

One of the primary goals of this book has been to increase appreciation and acknowledgment for the contribution of biblical women made in changing the world for the better. Their actions and their prophecies offer important guidance for people today. This book is, however, more than an accounting of inspiring teachings about the lives of Biblical women.

The loftiest goal of this book is to serve as a guidebook for the rise of the feminine spirit and the revelation of Godliness in the world so needed at this time. In each chapter, I highlight the unique feminine qualities embodied by each biblical woman along with meditations and spiritual practices to cultivate and enhance these qualities within ourselves. For there to be a true peace in our world, the deep inner feminine knowing of the sacredness and interconnectedness of life needs to be reclaimed and shared by both men and women alike. The voice of the feminine must be once again heard.

For there to be peace in our world, the harmony and balance between the masculine and feminine must be restored. This book is not for women alone. Men are also hungry for the heart and wisdom of their spiritual mothers as well.

Reclaiming the heart and wisdom of the feminine is a new phenomenon for many today. We are seeing hundreds of thousands of women of all faiths meet at the time of the new and full moon to share their visions, dreams, and prayers in a way that women might have done in ancient times. Not quite finding themselves spiritually or emotionally fulfilled in traditional patriarchal or even egalitarian religious settings, women today gather to explore alternative ways to create greater love, healing, and abundance in the world. It is my prayer that this book serve as a resource for these groups.

These female-only or female-led gatherings are significant because they foster an awakening to the ancient wisdom of the feminine. More importantly, they offer pathways for feminine empowerment beyond that of feminism. I recommend everyone being part of a female-only or female-led spiritual group. I personally have led alternative meditative gatherings for the Sabbath and Jewish holidays for over thirty years for men and women alike. Being a spiritual guide and teacher helped shape my deepening understanding of feminine spirituality.

Let us commit to celebrating and appreciating the differences between men and women. It was the Divine plan that the world be divided between masculine and feminine. Even God is dual gendered. Both genders are beautiful and necessary to each other. "God created man in His image, in the image of God He created him, male and female He created them" (Gen. 5:2).

Not only are there two genders, each person has masculine and feminine sensibilities within them. The values and wisdom of the feminine will have to rise to restore the balance needed for peace and harmony. To facilitate this harmony, individually and collectively, people must seek balance between the masculine and feminine energies within and between them. Doing versus being, achieving versus allowing, and spirituality versus physicality are just a few examples of the choices between the masculine and feminine people are confronted with today.

For many of us, harmony between the masculine and feminine within ourselves, our relationships, and our world, remains elusive. Too often, people today find their self-worth more in what they do more than who they are.

The masculine prowess of technology still has supremacy over the gentleness of the feminine heart and wisdom. Technology has expanded our communication. Most people in America have television, cell phones, and Internet. That is great. We can have frequent and instantaneous contact with each other. Technology serves an important purpose but it cannot replace the intimacy of being in the physical presence of another human being.

Technology is not the medium for authentic intimate communication. We must always remember that. Unfortunately, people today have social networks more than they have intimate loving families and communities where they can be authentic, vulnerable, and validated for who they are. The lack of real community contributes to widespread feelings of isolation, depression, and addiction. This deficit is due to the lack of honor given to the heart and wisdom of the feminine.

Since the advent of feminism, many women work out of the home not for economic reasons but for personal fulfillment. Feminism encouraged women to find fulfillment in their careers more than in their roles as mothers and homemakers. The many things that women traditionally did that provided for healing and nurturing for their families and communities have not been adequately appreciated.

Because of our lack of communities, women who stay at home as homemakers and mothers often feel isolated. I have met women who are even embarrassed to say they do not have a career. Bestowed with greater oxytocin (known as the love attachment hormone), women are natural nurturers. The important role women can play in fostering loving families and community must be better appreciated and honored by women and men.

It is a great privilege to be blessed to be a mother and wife. I wish I knew the depth of that when I was younger and my biological clock was still ticking. When will our society value the role that women play in making life more meaningful and harmonious? When will women validate themselves for the gifts they bring into the world simply by virtue of being women?

May it be soon. The world is in great need of the heart and wisdom of the feminine.

CONCLUDING BLESSINGS

Please take a few deep breaths, quiet your mind, and open your hearts to meditate on these affirmations. Receive the blessings that are contained within this book that I extend to you now with my full heart.

> *May I be inspired to reclaim the path of feminine spirituality that our biblical women so courageously walked. May I be blessed in unique ways to be strengthened by their examples.*

> *May these biblical women become so alive to me that I routinely ask myself, "What would Sarah do, what would Miriam say, when I have to make the choices that impact myself and others?" May my heart open so wide that I am filled with love for all of creation as the hearts of biblical women were.*

> *May I truly value the fullness and holiness of life itself over any abstract idealization or ideology as our biblical mothers did. May I have clear discernment like they did.*

> *May I be blessed to create holy sanctuaries in my homes, relationships, places of worship, and even in my own body where the Divine Presence can dwell, be known, revealed, and experienced.*

> *Amen selah.*

Whether you are a Jew or Christian, a woman or a man, your personal efforts are needed to make this world a dwelling place for God. The more we do towards this effort, the more we will be inspired to do, and the more joy and love we will be gifted to experience in our lives.

Let's hold the intention that in our heart and in actions we will reveal and embody the intrinsic Godliness that is at the heart of who we really are. We do not have to wait to do this. God is present right now. God is not just in heaven, but here on earth. That God realization is the heart and wisdom of the feminine. Right now, let us consciously choose to simply open our hearts and begin by creating opportunities to deepen intimate authentic connections between ourselves and others. This is the feminine way.

If ever you find yourself in an argument, if you find yourself criticizing a person, blaming another person for the feelings that have been triggered within you, please remember these holy words. "It is more important to be kind than right." These words are attributed to the Lubavitcher Rebbe, a great Jewish religious leader.

Repeat these words to yourself often when and if you find yourself angry with those close to you. It is easy to be right, but to be kind, you need to quiet the judgment of the ego-mind and open your heart more deeply. In that quiet place within yourself, you will find God. This is the feminine way. Be kind. Be generous. Kindness and generosity are the basis for all good relationships. Know that if you are angry, you block the revelation of God within you. This takes the greatest toll on you. Illness is often rooted in these blockages.

Being compassionate and engaging in acts of love and kindness is healing to everyone, the giver and the receiver. When we are kind, we are gifted with a joyful awareness of the intrinsic unity within all of life. Our words and our deeds may inspire others to also be kind and loving. The more kindness, the greater receptivity there is to the higher frequencies of the Divine.

The light of God burns within very person. As the Talmud says, "The light of a candle can light many candles without its own light being diminished." In all of our own relationships, we can demonstrate the heart and wisdom of the feminine. This is not a small thing. It makes a huge difference. We do not and cannot do this work alone.

When the masculine and feminine in this world and on high is balanced, there will be peace and well-being. This Jewish teaching is expressed in the blessings recited after every meal of a newly wedded couple. May we continue to walk in the footsteps of our biblical mothers to restore balance in this world.

POSTSCRIPT

Always feel free to visit my website www.kabbalahoftheheart.com and contact me at miriam@Kabbalahoftheheart.com or Ribner@msn.com Sign up for my monthly newsletter on the Kabbalistic energies of the months, holidays, meditation, healing, etc.

If you are interested in further integrating and applying the wisdom of the heart of the feminine into your life or in the practice of Kabbalistic meditation, please email me. If you are part of a woman's group, and you would like to study this material in the book further so as to deepen the experience of feminine spirituality within the group, please contact me. There is so much more that I have to teach and transmit about the feminine that could not be contained within the confines of the written word. I would love to hear from you. Please feel free to write me and post reviews on Amazon.

I hope that you will share this book with the members of your community. If invited, I will come to share with your community. I have prepared a number of dynamic lectures and workshops around the women and teachings in the book. Contact me for an online brochure of offerings.

Before your very eyes, I will become each biblical woman in a theatrical performance in person or online.

www.ingramcontent.com/pod-product-compliance
Lightning Source LLC
Chambersburg PA
CBHW021148080526
44588CB00008B/261